SpringerBriefs

Key Thinkers in Education

Series editor

Paul Gibbs, London, UK

This briefs series publishes compact (50 to 125 pages) refereed monographs under the editorial supervision of the Advisory Editor, Professor Paul Gibbs, Middlesex University, Nicosia, Cyprus. Each volume in the series provides a concise introduction to the life and work of a key thinker in education and allows readers to get acquainted with their major contributions to educational theory and/or practice in a fast and easy way.

More information about this series at http://www.springer.com/series/10197

Tony Wall · David Perrin

Slavoj Žižek

A Žižekian Gaze at Education

 Springer

Tony Wall
Centre for Work Related Studies
University of Chester
Chester
UK

David Perrin
Centre for Work Related Studies
University of Chester
Chester
UK

ISSN 2211-1921   ISSN 2211-193X   (electronic)
SpringerBriefs in Education
ISSN 2211-937X   ISSN 2211-9388   (electronic)
SpringerBriefs on Key Thinkers in Education
ISBN 978-3-319-21241-8   ISBN 978-3-319-21242-5   (eBook)
DOI 10.1007/978-3-319-21242-5

Library of Congress Control Number: 2015943048

Springer Cham Heidelberg New York Dordrecht London

Printed on acid-free paper

Springer International Publishing AG Switzerland is part of Springer Science+Business Media
(www.springer.com)

A wise French elder once said "les non-dupes errent". People are always tricking themselves, and when we entertain the idea that this might possibly apply to you and I, new ways of thinking and acting can appear. The task is then to figure out which route to take.

To Slavoj Žižek who continues to create havoc.
To Tony Brown for introducing me to these ideas.
To Ian Barron who questioned why I should bother.
To The Walls who kept my home warm in the winter as a child.

Dr. Tony Wall
New York
March 2015

To the learners of the world—you have nothing to lose but your aims (learning outcomes and credits).

Dr. David Perrin
Chester
March 2015

Contents

Abbreviations

AQF	Australian Qualifications Framework
CATS	Credit Accumulation and Transfer System
DLHE	Destinations of Leavers from Higher Education Survey
ECTS	European Credit Transfer (and accumulation) System
FCA	Financial Conduct Authority
FE	Further Education
FHEQ	Framework for Higher Education Qualifications
HE	Higher Education
HEFCE	Higher Education Funding Council for England
HEFCW	Higher Education Funding Council for Wales
HESA	Higher Education Statistics Agency
HKQF	Hong Kong Qualifications Framework
KIS	Key Information Sets
MOOC	Massive Open Online Course
NOS	National Occupational Standards
NQF	National Qualifications Framework
NUS	National Union of Students
OER	Open Educational Resources
OFSTED	The Office for Standards in Education
OIA	Office of the Independent Adjudicator for Higher Education
QCF	Qualifications & Credit Framework
SFA	Skills Funding Agency
TAFE	Technical and Further Education
UCU	Universities and Colleges Union
WEA	Workers' Education Association
WSQ	Workforce Skills Qualifications (Singapore)

Chapter 1
Introduction

Slavoj Žižek has been called, amongst other things, the "Elvis of cultural theory", the "Foucault of Our Time" (Wallace 1998) and listed as one of Foreign Policy magazine's Top 100 Global Thinkers. His rise to fame began as an active Slovenian 'leftist' during the 1980s, but his crown was firmly secured with the publication of *The Sublime Object of Ideology* (1989) along with prolific writing and media attention. Today, armed with the same Marxist commitments and animated, unorthodox flair, he continues to attract major acclaim and criticism from across the globe. It is not surprising that, so the story goes, that tickets to a Žižek gig sold out faster than a Michael Jackson gig in London.

Žižek rarely speaks about education directly, but his ideas are appearing more and more in the context of scholarly commentaries on educational policy (for example, Cooley 2009) as well as emancipatory forms of teacher action research (for example, Brown et al. 2006; Brown and McNamara 2011; Meakin and Wall 2013; Wall 2013). Scholars have described Žižek's thinking as "iconoclastic" (Cooley 2009, p. 381), with an ambition to provoke us into considering how contemporary capitalism works to shape how we think, feel and act in ways that we may not even notice. If we think education and educational opportunities may be progressing, he wants us to pay attention to claims such as these (Žižek 2014, p. 17):

> Never has there been less hunger, less disease or more prosperity... Globalisation means the world's not just getting richer, but fairer too...the forces of peace, progress and prosperity are prevailing. (The Spectator 2012)

He urges us to examine the *troubles* in our so called *paradise*, or the antagonisms that exist and are created by the particular ways of operating that become naturalised or taken-for-granted in our educational settings. As Žižek says, the task is to "not simply accept what exists as given... but raise the question of how is what we encounter as actual also possible" (Žižek 1993, p. 2). Contemporary capitalism has done its work when we become 'excessively close' to particular ways of thinking, and as such, generates a cycle of 'familiarity breeds consent' (Taylor 2010, p. 9).

© The Author(s) 2015
T. Wall and D. Perrin, *Slavoj Žižek*,
SpringerBriefs on Key Thinkers in Education,
DOI 10.1007/978-3-319-21242-5_1

It is not difficult to find these troubles in contemporary education: Why do we have record levels of student complaints and compensation in higher education? What is compelling our students to become disgruntled when they do not receive great customer service or good grades? Why are our school and university teachers so stressed? Why is it so difficult to create radical change in educational contexts? These are the symptoms of the trouble in paradise that Žižek wants us to notice, explore and explode.

For Žižek, however, this is not just about awareness: contrary to the Marxist dictum 'we know not what we do', Žižek exclaims 'we do know what we do, but still do it!'. This book aspires to provide an interpretation of Žižekian ideas as applied to education, which is still a scant area. However, as we will see, it does so without attempting to capture the totality of Žižek or his ideas, which would be an impossible ambition. Rather, it aims to capture partial glimpses, enough to inspire additional readings, thinking—and most importantly, action—of the reader.

This is the first book that focuses on the application of Žižekian thought to educational contexts. It attempts to be accessible in the main, so is designed to be read from cover to cover, each chapter building on the previous. That said, to dip into the book at various points will give you a flavour of Žižekian ideas as we interpret them, as well as some of the concerns that such ideas conjure. However, some parts of the book will be easier to read than others—this mirrors the experience of reading Žižek's work: sometimes it is useful to read and re-read specific parts and even seek out other texts related to certain aspects of his work.

The book is structured as follows. The second chapter is a broad introduction to Žižekian thought, style and approach. Here, we lay the foundations of some of the key ideas we think Žižek puts to work, including Marx, Lacan and Hegel—ideas and tactics which create supporters and detractors alike. In the third chapter, we illustrate contemporary understandings of education, which leads us into discussions about one of the key dimensions of Žižek's theoretical tools, the Symbolic (that is, how language is used to shape how we construct our reality).

In the fourth chapter, we explore how these constructs implicate those in education, including teachers and students alike, and have an insidious role in mobilising unconscious desires and drives. These constructs have a powerful role in activating how we think we should act in educational practice, and explain how, with reference to the other two dimensions of Žižek's theoretical tools, the Imaginary realm and the Real.

Combined, these three dimensions (the Symbolic, the Imaginary, the Real) work together in and out of awareness to keep us firmly in their grip. We discuss this in more detail in Chap. 5, which explores how we can know about our troubles in our so-called paradise, but carry on regardless. Though powerful, we can also utilise these mechanics to explore and experiment with other ways of engaging in our educational realities, the focus of our penultimate chapter. We hope this book acts as a springboard to learning more about Žižek and his ideas, and we provide some additional advice and ideas within the final chapter of the book. As Boynton (1998) once said, we hope you *"Enjoy Your Žižek!"*.

References

Boynton, R. S. (1998). Enjoy Your Zizek! an excitable Slovenian Philosopher examines the obscene practices of everyday life—Including his own. *Linguafranca: The Review of Academic Life, 8*(7).

Brown, T., Atkinson, D., & England, J. (2006). *Regulative discourses in education: A Lacanian perspective*. London: Peter Lang publishers.

Brown, T., & McNamara, O. (2011). *Becoming a mathematics teacher: Identity and identifications*. Dordrecht: Springer.

Cooley, A. (2009). Is education a lost cause? Žižek, schooling, and universal emancipation. *Discourse: Studies in the Cultural Politics of Education,30*(4), 381–395.

Meakin, D., & Wall, T. (2013). Co-delivered work based learning: Contested ownership and responsibility. *Higher Education, Skills & Work Based Learning,3*(1), 73–81.

Taylor, P. (2010). *Žižek and the Media*. Cambridge: Polity Press.

The Spectator. (2012). The spectator—Glad tidings. http://www.spectator.co.uk/the-week/leading-article/8789981/glad-tidings/.

Wall, T. (2013). *Professional identities and commodification in higher education*. Unpublished Doctoral Thesis, Manchester Metropolitan University, Manchester.

Wallace, J. (1998). *Times higher education—Foucault of our time*. Retrieved March 14, 2015, from http://www.timeshighereducation.co.uk/110089.article.

Žižek, S. (1989). *The sublime object of ideology*. London: Verso.

Žižek, S. (1993). *Tarrying with the negative: Kant, Hegel, and the critique of ideology*. Durham: Duke University Press.

Žižek, S. (2014). *Trouble in paradise: From the end of history to the end of capitalism*. London: Allen Lane.

Chapter 2
Welcome to Žižek's Beard

Abstract The problems and possibilities of educating in ways that enable people to break free from their shackles continues to exercise critical educationalists. This is where Žižek takes his stage as a skilled provocateur; he is notoriously difficult to read and is criticised for speaking through excessive storytelling and exemplification of points, often without actually stating what his point is (or might be). With a dialectical twist, however, here is Žižek in his full pedagogical glory, sharing important learning opportunities with us; it is us who have to take an active role in making sense of what 'the point' is, and what to do with it once we think we have grasped it. Žižek thinks, writes and performs like a cocktail with a kick: a Marxist liquid base, mixed with a dash of Lacan and Hegel on the rocks. The result is a commitment to tackling and navigating a contemporary capitalist society in ways which expose the hidden tricks and illusions that mobilise our deep unconscious motivations, often in contradictory ways. Never with a clear solution in sight, these underpinnings form a kind of Žižekian critical pedagogy; a way of engaging us in thinking about education without set or prescribed answers, but with crucial questions that take us on intellectual rollercoasters of inquiry about what education might involve, and therefore what it might become. But Žižek warns us, every perspective can only ever be partial, so bearing this in mind, welcome to our story of Žižek's beard.

Keywords Marx · Lacan · Hegel · Ideology · Situationist · Provocation · Critical

What Do You Get When You Mix Marx with Lacan and Hegel?

There is a not so well known joke about Žižek which serves the purpose of introducing this book and the man himself in a fully affectionate fashion. Two academics travel to London for a talk about 'how to start a social revolution in

© The Author(s) 2015
T. Wall and D. Perrin, *Slavoj Žižek*,
SpringerBriefs on Key Thinkers in Education,
DOI 10.1007/978-3-319-21242-5_2

30 minutes'. They enter a large, poorly lit lecture theatre that can seat over 300 eager students. They choose to sit on the front row so they can see the presenter clearly and easily read the presentation slides. The lecture theatre soon fills up with the prospect of learning something insightful from the celebrity speaker; it is such a popular talk that people are standing on the rickety staircase alongside the multiple rows of seats. As the two academics wait with silent enthusiasm, the half-hearted spotlights fail and the audience plunges into complete darkness.

The two academics tentatively leave their seats and stumble forward. Fumbling around, they try their best to reach for a light switch or to open a door to shed light into the blackness. After rummaging in the dark, the first academic finds an object which is prickly, stiff and dry, much like the bristles of a garden brush. He wonders why there is such an object in the lecture theatre. The second academic reaches out and carefully handles a soft and thin fabric, much like the texture of an under-garment fit for the harshness of winter. He, like the first academic, wonders why there is such an object in the lecture theatre. Soon enough, the lights flick on to full beam with startling brightness. There, revealed in full colour and fiercely vivid, are the two academics fondling two parts of Žižek; one was grasping his t-shirt, and the other was groping his beard.

There is of course another version of the joke that starts with 'two academics walk into a bar…', but the ending is pretty much the same. Both jokes are a useful introduction to a book about Žižek's ideas and how they might be useful to people working in education. To the cynical eye, for example, the humorous aspects of the joke would not have been the fondling of Žižek's bits. It might have been the contemporary impossibility of there being 300 students sat in a lecture theatre (rather than being in bed). Or the unlikely nature of there being 300 students interested in starting a social revolution—in whatever timeframe. Another aspect might have been the contemporary educational condition where educationalists are required to package up their knowledge into specific consumable forms, in this case, 'how to start a social revolution in 30 minutes'. That is of course, avoiding the possibility of the question 'how many academics does it take to change a light bulb?'.

For a Žižekian gaze, however, these are not just flippant comments about a joke: they provide Marxist glimpses into contemporary issues in education in modern capitalist society. For Žižek, Marx exerts such an "influence in the general field of social sciences… offering us a key to the theoretical understanding of phenomena… [where] there is definitely more at stake than the commodity form" (Žižek 1994, p. 301). By this, Žižek is referring to how our sense of reality is shaped when production in society takes the form of an "immense collection of commodities" (Marx 1976, p. 73) where articles of wealth are bought and sold in the market. Here, we develop a commodity fetish, whereby we attribute to the product being exchanged something which is *more than* the commodities being exchanged, and *more than* the social relations that are involved in the making and exchanging of them. Something 'mystical' beyond the physical commodity which captures us in ways where we have deep desires for these things, such as big cars or houses (even though these might not of themselves be accurate measures of wealth). For Marx, this was a 'false consciousness', or a distortion of a self or being, that was based on something other than a 'natural' way of being.

Our problem in this context is that this false consciousness feels real; a consciousness distorted by a particular way of being, or particular "doctrine, composite of ideas, beliefs, concepts..." (Žižek 1999, p. 63), or ideology. The conventional Marxist concern is that these ideological grips take hold because 'we do not know what we do', until we do become aware of it and revolt in some way, morphing the capitalist society into something else—hence the emancipatory flavour of Žižek's work, with commitments to social revolution and change (Butler 2005; Taylor 2010; Wood 2012). Yet Žižek is intensely interested in why 'we *do* know what we do, *and still do it...*' (Žižek 1989). To explain this, he often refers to that well known amateur philosopher Donald Rumsfeld, the then US Secretary of Defense, to elaborate on the dangers we face:

> 'There are known knowns; there are things we know that we know. There are known unknowns; that is to say, there are things that we now know we don't know. But there are also unknown unknowns – there are things we do not know we don't know.'... But what Rumsfeld forgot to add was the crucial fourth term: the 'unknown knowns', the things we don't know that we know –... which is precisely the Freudian unconscious... a symbolically articulated knowledge ignored by the subject... [which] frame, of our experience of reality. (Žižek 2014, pp. 8–10)

Žižek wants us to seek out and closely examine these 'unknown knows', because they alert us to how contemporary capitalism manifests in our daily lives, despite our awareness of it. It is for this intense concern, scholars say that Žižek offers "iconoclastic interpretation of the ubiquitous and deeply naturalised nature of ideology today... min[ing] the (only apparently) obvious and prosaic in order to produce startling insights" (Taylor 2010, p. 3).

It is here where he employs the psychoanalytical apparatus of Lacan, particularly Lacan's later theoretical expositions of the Borromean knot, as a metaphor for the mechanics of human subjectivity (Myers 2003; Wood 2012; Žižek 2014). The dimensions of the Borromean knot (for Lacan, the Symbolic and Imaginary realms and the Real) and how they interconnect will be the focus of the rest of this book, but a key insight here is that the language we use on a daily basis is by no means innocent, but always loaded with particular ways of engaging with the world—and it is these which shape how we engage in education, and in any sphere of life (also see Barnett (2003, 2011) in the context of education). With these tools, Žižek explains how particular ways of thinking and relating to things within capitalist society live through our language and influence how we act in daily situations. But as we will soon see, in what is quintessentially Žižek, it is not just what is captured by language that shapes us, *but also that which escapes it has importance to our unconscious desires and drives.* And this is central to why we might notice 'troubles in paradise' but carry on regardless, even if we have been trained to question our own assumptions and engage in critical reflection—we are readily duped and tricked, and 'being critical' can even lead to the concepts we are seeking to dismantle taking an even tighter grip on us (Žižek 2006).

This helps to explain why Žižek uses, some would say excessively relies upon, stories and jokes to illuminate and animate his ideas. In one reading of his approach, we might argue that much of his writing is not necessarily direct or clear in the point he is making (see some of the critiques at the end of this chapter). Yet in another reading, this repetitive storytelling is about illuminating aspects, dimensions or angles of the point he is trying to make, rather than being absolutely, definitively clear about what the point is: his argument is that as soon as we try to capture some-thing, something else always escapes. Just like in the joke at the start of this chapter, it is a situation of: is it a garden brush? Is it an undergarment? No, it's Žižek! Sometimes, Žižek's jokes or stories can be considered vulgar or low class. The intention here seems to be to shake, shock, jolt or move the way we see the things and acts around us that are taken for granted, that is, that have become naturalised (the unknown knowns). He says:

> Most people think I'm making jokes, exaggerating – but no, I'm not. It's not that. First I tell jokes, then I'm serious. No, the art is to bring the serious message into the forum of jokes. (Aitkenhead 2012)

Elsewhere he argues that "fiction is more real than the social reality of playing roles" (Žižek 2001, p. 75) because "there is a domain of fantasmatic intimacy which is marked by a "No Trespass!" sign" (Žižek 2001, p. 72). In other words, our attitude of engagement with something that is marked as 'fiction' allows us to see aspects or dimensions of a situation that we would not normally want to see. As we will discover later on, it might be deeply unsettling to who we think we are if we do see it directly (or might give us a headache), even though it is present in our behaviour.

The jokes and stories are aspects of Žižek's provocations and he sits within a long tradition of provocateurs. His startling interventions (and possibly motivations) have parallels with the Situationists who emerged in the late 1950s and attracted a certain vogue around the time of the events in Paris a decade or so later. Theirs was an anti-authoritarian Marxism which involved the attempt to influence and construct unsettling 'situations', from the small-scale such as squatting and the disfiguring of advertising hoardings, to the large-scale 'May Events' in Paris of 1968 (see Debord 1970; Vaneigem 1983). The idea was to challenge the ways in which our commodity fetish was taking hold in our daily lives, in order to enable people to free their desires, and go beyond the prevalent wage labour-money-commodity relationships. As Vaneigem implied, workers' relationships with the means of consumption were becoming almost as significant as their relationship to the means of production:

> Purchasing power is a license to purchase power. The old proletariat sold its labour power in order to subsist; what little leisure time it had was passed pleasantly enough in conversations, arguments, drinking, making love, wandering, celebrating and rioting. The new proletarian sells his labour power in order to consume. When he's not flogging himself to death to get promoted in the labour hierarchy, he's being persuaded to buy himself objects to distinguish himself in the social hierarchy. (Vaneigem 1983, p. 52)

The Situationists strongly influenced some of the founders of the punk rock phenomenon in the mid-1970s, including Malcolm McLaren, manager of the Sex Pistols (Marcus 1989). The notorious foul-mouthed appearance by the Sex Pistols on ITV's live Bill Grundy show in 1976 was an act of cultural sabotage and provocation reflecting the dictum 'we still have some time to take advantage of the fact that radio and television stations are not yet guarded by the army' (Debord 1970). Their deliberately ripped clothing, safety pins and bondage trousers were purposively designed to challenge contemporary conceptions of fashion and therefore to shock. In many ways, their working-class youthful insouciance reflected a conscious desire to provoke the consumers of suburbia into questioning received nostrums and conventional behaviours. This aspiration also motivated their re-appropriation of the swastika and portraits of Karl Marx—especially given they were certainly not Nazis, and not necessarily Marxists either.

Though it may not be immediately obvious that this reflects a Žižekian style, is this not precisely what Žižek does to make things even more eye-caching and exciting (or perhaps frustrating for some)? Indeed, is this not what he is doing in his provocative display of pictures of Stalin in his home (Taylor 2005)? In his scholarly work, Žižek has been known to engage in 'literary hoaxes', for example, publishing fictional roundtable discussions, and an intentionally flawed critique on an imaginary book (Boynton 1998). Perhaps there is an intention to encourage an attitude of engaging in and questioning the debate rather than consuming it? Or perhaps it was a statement about the 'unknown knowns' of academic publishing systems? In our view, this sort of approach is about placing a 'question mark' over what we are reading or hearing, which is an invitation to possibly do both, more, and possibly neither. Sir Ken Robinson might agree with the spirit of Žižek's ambition to offer forms of teaching and learning which enable new creative capacities to flourish in education, rather than 'kill it', if not, perhaps the vehicle and tactics Žižek uses (see TED 2015).

This leads to another aspect of a Žižekian gaze on education: the close examination of antagonisms also feature in Žižek's work through the use of contradiction, using a dialectical method. Žižek illustrates this pointedly in *Event* where he observes 'take away the illusion and you lose the truth itself' (2014, p. 106). In other words, it is through opposition and polarity that real meaning can be found and (potentially) progress can occur. Inspired by Hegel, with a dash of Marx and Lacan, Žižek considers that everything contains the seeds of its own transcendence, or every paradise has with it, troubles. Here, every 'thing' has opposing elements in a shifting and unstable equilibrium that can burst asunder and create a new formation when the composition of the elements changes. Hegel's dialectical approach —often simplified into thesis/antithesis/synthesis—was famously adapted and refined by Marx who attempted to relocate its driving force from the abstract realm of ideas to the notion of ideas being situated in (and driven by) particular circumstances. Hence Marx's comment:

Men make their own history, but they do not make it just as they please, they do not make it under circumstances chosen by themselves, but under circumstances directly encountered, given, and transmitted from the past. (Marx 1984, p. 360)

It is through opposition and polarity in these circumstances, Žižek argues, that we can find new insights into how contemporary capitalism works and how it can trick us into repeating and reproducing it. At a fundamental level these Žižekian moves are attempts to encourage 'sense-making' through highlighting and emphasising contradictions and questioning the assumptions which set them up, within the context of specific daily circumstances or situations. And the practical application of this method—as with Lacan—involves word-play, jokes, puns, and much else that can expose hidden contradictions and encourage alternative perspectives, identifying and magnifying the unstable elements of the dialectical process so as to establish movement towards a new, unstable equilibrium. This Žižekian frame and method applies to education as well as much else—indeed, in many ways *what we learn, how we learn it and for what ends*, is at the very heart of Žižek's philosophical approach, and in this respect his method has an intrinsic epistemological dimension.

Žižek might well have been an avid punk rocker (or of course, the converse: punk rockers might well have the full and extensive Žižek back catalogue), but perhaps his leanings position him somewhat closer to contemporaries like Frank Furedi, an educational scholar with similar, self-consciously controversial stances that garner media attention? It is no surprise that Furedi has a comparable academic and radical background: Furedi was the leading theoretician of one of Britain's erstwhile Trotskyist organisations (the Revolutionary Communist Party), and was then part of the network of provocative media commentators and academics that emerged from it (Spiked Ltd 2015). From his support for Argentina in the Falklands War to recent opposition to state censorship disguised as anti-terrorism legislation, Furedi seems to demonstrate similar influences and methods.

For both Žižek and Furedi, provocation and polarity are defining threads. So this leads us towards our answer to the question, 'what do you get when an educationalist mixes up Marx, Lacan and Hegel?'. The answer is probably 'an emancipatory hagfish pedagogy', but this needs some explaining. The hag fish has an inbuilt property whereby as soon as it is pressed or grasped, it releases a slimy substance which repels or resists its capture. This is not a claim that Žižek or his approach is fishy or slimy in any literal sense, but the hag fish and its properties provide an angle from which to think about and make sense of Žižek and his ways of educating (or provoking). In engaging with Žižek, there is always a sense of not fully capturing what he is saying, because he is circling the point with a recognition that as soon as he tries to capture it precisely, something escapes (an utterly Lacanian point).

With such a frustrating approach, the responsibility of sense making becomes a task for the audience: we have to understand the possible messages in statements and interactions, rather than relying on the communicator to specifically outline what is intended (and of course, the associated exertions of power in such a relationship). This, for Žižek, is a starting point to generating new ways to act, or at the very least, raising the possibility of new ways to act.

The same applies to this book; as we attempt to become increasingly precise about what Žižek and his ideas are, there will be an inevitable failure. We might grasp his beard and his t-shirt through this book, and they might feel like something very real to us as we grasp at them—but a bit of Žižek will always escape. Yet this inevitable failure is not a unique feature of this book, but any book about Žižek and his work: none of these books grasp the totality of Žižek. This is perhaps what stimulates the International Journal of Žižek Studies and its vibrant community of over 14,000 subscribers across multiple fields. There are not enough hands to grasp the totality of Žižek within this book, but using Žižekian thought, we realise that would be an impossible task. All we can aim to do is reveal a part of his beard and expose a bit of the t-shirt, in ways that may be interesting to people working (or studying) within the education system.

Lovers and Haters

There is a well-known yeast extract product which is the by-product of beer-brewing. Its intensely salty flavour and dark gloopy texture splits opinion— some people love it, and some absolutely detest it. It seems Žižek creates the same effect, as captured by this critical question: "Is [Žižek] an intellectual charlatan who has parlayed his neurosis and love of film into academic celebrity?" (Cooley 2009, p. 382). Žižek receives criticism about his style (including lack of academic refer- encing in many of his pieces), approach, as well as theoretical underpinnings. Many of Žižek's most trenchant critics have especially attacked his method as philo- sophical agent provocateur, claiming that this has allowed him to hide behind a lack of specificity in his outlook. In effect, a method that has led him to be labelled a theorist without any theory, an empty vessel making much philosophical 'noise'.

Perhaps most notably, this has been the line adopted by Noam Chomsky, another self-styled radical theorist who has set about challenging a wide variety of cherished assumptions about capitalism and how it operates:

> [W]hen I said I'm not interested in theory, what I meant is, I'm not interested in posturing – using fancy terms like polysyllables and pretending you have a theory when you have no theory whatsoever. So there's no theory in any of this stuff, not in the sense of theory that anyone is familiar with in the sciences or any other serious field. Try to find in all of the work you mentioned some principles from which you can deduce conclusions, empirically testable propositions where it all goes beyond the level of something you can explain in five minutes to a twelve-year-old. See if you can find that when the fancy words are decoded. I can't. So I'm not interested in that kind of posturing. Žižek is an extreme example of it. (Chomsky in Veterans Unplugged 2015)

There have been other trenchant critics in the anti-capitalist and anti-globalisation movements too. On occasion, these have contended that Žižek's method has effectively hidden or obscured an authoritarianism seemingly out of keeping with his otherwise radical posturing (Roos 2013). Some might argue his approach which explores inversions and sets up contradictions 'does not make sense at all' (Cooley 2009; Myers 2003). Or, simply put, it is "impenetrable" (Aitkenhead 2012). Another theoretical criticism relates to the extent to which we are shaped by the wider social structures in which we participate. For example, some have argued that psychoanalysis generally (not Žižek specifically) over-emphasises these determinants and does not provide sufficient wiggle room for an individual to "escape complete and utter domination and compliance" (Holland et al. 1998, p. 32). For Holland et al.:

> persons develop through and around the cultural forms by which they are identified, and identify themselves, in the context of their affiliation or disaffiliation with those associated with those forms and practices. A better metaphor for us is not suture, which makes the person and the position seem to arrive preformed at the moment of suturing, but co-development – the linked development of people, cultural forms, and social positions in particular historical worlds. (Holland et al. 1998, pp. 32–33)

This book will encourage you to consider and develop your own views, which we hope might mean exploring Žižek's work and his opponents in more depth (see the final chapter of this book for springboards into other resources). However, many scholars have sensed in Žižek's work a fundamental desire to shift thinking beyond the conventional and towards the transformative. We align with Cooley who argues:

> it is clear that Žižek's work is useful in the sense that is has the hallmark of all great philosophy – namely it raises questions about people's beliefs and concentrates on aspects of everyday life... Žižek can be seen as a modern gadfly uttering the ancient Socratic mantra 'the unexamined life is not worth living' within the media and cultural spectacle of the present. (Cooley 2009, p. 382)

Or as Aitkenhead says, he operates with:

> exhilarating ambition and his central thesis offers a perspective even his critics would have to concede is thought-provoking. In essence, he argues that nothing is ever what it appears, and contradiction is encoded in almost everything. Most of what we think of as radical or subversive – or even simply ethical – doesn't actually change anything. (Aitkenhead 2012)

Our view is that if Žižek is having the same polarising effect as a yeast extract product—in his case, to spark lively debate about contemporary events—this is a productive activity for social change that can be aligned to Marxist ambitions. For us, Žižek is often true to his theoretical underpinnings (as discussed above), and there is always the possibility of a Žižekian intention to disrupt with almost every statement he makes, especially the ones which deeply offend (see for example, Schuman 2014). What we value from a Žižekian style and approach is the possibility of feeling effected and inspired to act in some way, but with the possibility of our setting our own next steps through the thick, yeasty substance. Žižek very rarely talks about education directly. It is our view that a Žižekian frame applies to education as well as much else and enables us to make comments about what we learn, how we learn it and for what ends. So how do these ideas and methods relate to education more specifically? This is where our focus now turns.

References

Aitkenhead, D. (2012). *The Guardian - Slavoj Žižek: 'Humanity is OK, but 99 % of people are boring idiots'*. Retrieved March 14, 2015, from http://www.theguardian.com/culture/2012/jun/10/slavoj-zizek-humanity-ok-people-boring.

Barnett, R. (2003). *Beyond all reason: Living with ideology in the University*. London: Society for Research into Higher Education.

Barnett, R. (2011). The coming of the ecological University. *Oxford Review of Education, 37*(4), 439–455.

Boynton, R. S. (1998). Enjoy your Zizek! an excitable Slovenian Philosopher examines the obscene practices of everyday life—Including his own. *Lingufranca: The Review of Academic Life, 8*(7).

Butler, R. (2005). *Slavoj Žižek: Live Theory*. London: Continuum.

Cooley, A. (2009). Is education a lost cause? Žižek, schooling, and universal emancipation. *Discourse: Studies in the Cultural Politics of Education, 30*(4), 381–395.

Debord, G. (1970). *Society of the spectacle*. London: Black and Red.

Holland, D., Lachiocotte, W., Skinner, D., & Cain, C. (1998). *Identity and agency in cultural worlds*. Cambridge, MA: Harvard University Press.

Marcus, G. (1989). *Lipstick traces*. London: Secker and Warburg.

Marx, K. (1976). *Capital* (Vol. 1). Harmondsworth: Penguin.

Marx, K. (1984). The eighteenth Brumaire of Louis Napoleon. In K. Marx & F. Engels (Eds.), *Basic writings on philosophy and politics* (pp. 358–388). Aylesbury: Fontana/Collins.

Myers, T. (2003). *Žižek*. London: Routledge Critical Thinkers.

Roos, J. (2013). *Roarmag.org—The dangerous dreams of Slavoj Žižek*. Retrieved March 16, 2015, from http://roarmag.org/2013/04/zizek-indignados-occupy-direct-democracy-critique/.

Schuman, R. (2014). *Slate—Please stop worshipping the superstar Professor who calls students "Boring Idiots"*. Retrieved March 14, 2015, from http://www.slate.com/blogs/browbeat/2014/06/02/slavoj_zizek_calls_students_stupid_and_boring_stop_worshiping_this_man_video.html.

Spiked Ltd. (2015). *Spiked online*. Retrieved February 13, 2015, from http://www.spiked-online.com/.

Taylor, A. (2005). *Žižek! [DVD]*. London: Institute of contemporary arts films.

Taylor, P. (2010). *Žižek and the Media*. Cambridge: Polity Press.

TED. (2015). *Sir Ken Robinson*. Retrieved March 12, 2015, from http://www.ted.com/speakers/sir_ken_robinson.

Vaneigem, R. (1983). *Revolution of everyday life*. London: Left Bank Books/Rebel Press.

Veterans Unplugged. (2015). *"Virtual Town Hall" Interview with Noam Chomsky from December 2012*. Retrieved February 18, 2015, from http://veteransunplugged.com/theshow/archive/118-chomsky-december-2012.

Wood, K. (2012). *Zizek: A reader's guide*. London: Wiley.

Žižek, S. (1989). *The sublime object of ideology*. London: Verso.

Žižek, S. (1994). How did Marx invent the symptom? In S. Žižek (Ed.), *Mapping ideology* (pp. 296–331). London: Verso.

Žižek, S. (1999). The spectre of ideology. In E. Wright & E. Wright (Eds.), *The Žižek Reader*. Malden, MA: Blackwell.

Žižek, S. (2001). *The fright of real tears: Krzysztof Kieslowski between theory and post-theory*. Bloomington: Indiana University Press.

Žižek, S. (2006). *The parallax view*. Cambridge, MA: MIT Press.

Žižek, S. (2014). *Event*. London: Penguin.

Chapter 3
Which Education?

Abstract To take a Žižekian gaze at education, we are invited to try on a pair of 'critico-ideological' glasses which help us to look awry at our educational life, and notice the taken-for-granted things around us. Though these glasses are not available in all good opticians, they are valuable in helping us see that things are not what they seem, and as we will see later, there are troubling consequences for all involved. Žižek urges us to use these glasses to examine the hidden forces at play in educational contexts, specifically, how we draw from the Symbolic realm, that is, how we try to represent or capture things in our educational realities. This gives us useful insights into how we are making sense of education, but also how we activate particular coordinates of how we think we should act in practice. When we try on these glasses and gaze at education, we do not need to look far to see how contemporary education across all sectors is understood in terms of economic utility, and as such, how this shapes how people relate and engage. Žižek warns, however, that "when one looks for too long at reality through critico-ideological glasses, one gets a strong headache" (Žižek 2013): we might not like what we see as it might have devastating effects on how we see the world and on how we see ourselves. The paradox is that this headache is simultaneously the source of creating new ways forward, as we will soon see.

Keywords Economic utility · The symbolic · Antagonism · Bureaucracy

Education 'Best Buys'

Let us imagine a contemporary, practical, scenario to illuminate a Žižekian concern: your daughter reaches the stage in life where she needs to choose a university. Turning to the web and social media, she begins to access detailed reviews of higher education providers and courses. She scrolls down a list of reviews available on a popular consumer choice website, scrolling down a list of reviews for vacuum cleaners, televisions, computers, cars, ovens, cameras, irons, where to give birth to a child, and so on. She pauses temporarily to have a quick look at reviews of care

© The Author(s) 2015   15
T. Wall and D. Perrin, *Slavoj Žižek*,
SpringerBriefs on Key Thinkers in Education,
DOI 10.1007/978-3-319-21242-5_3

providers for her elderly parents (you), and then continues scrolling. Eventually, she finds the link for higher education courses and clicks. Here, she carefully selects her requirements from a 'drop down' box listing multiple options, where she chooses her academic subject major, combination subject minor, professional body accreditations, geographic location, price, duration of course, and so on.

She examines multiple rankings, including national and international rankings, and rankings specifically related to teaching quality, research quality and employability prospects. She reads rankings related to how beautiful the campus is, how good the food is on campus, sportiness of classmates, as well the quality of student parties and the levels of alcohol and drugs consumed. The website generates a list of the perfect course which matches her detailed requirements.

Is this a vulgar exaggeration? No: higher education courses are now reviewed alongside 1,000s of consumer goods on popular consumer choice and product review magazine websites to enable the customer to make a well informed choice (for example, see Which.com). Now, higher education is juxtaposed alongside the sorts of advertisements we see to increase the sale of goods like a coffee machine. One site had an advert similar to this:

> Coffee making machines: Click here to find the latest coffee machines from the best brands! Find our 15 *Best Purchase* reviews that recommend the smoothest coffee with the most fragrant scents. Read our top 50 chart and search all of our 150 reviews to find your perfect coffee maker – and don't miss our 'To Avoid' reviews! All for an irresistible 99p trial!

Are we surprised, then, that we might even see advertisements like this:

> Degree: Click here to find the latest degree courses from the best universities! Find our 15 *Best Purchase* reviews that recommend the universities with the highest employability rates. Read our top 50 chart and search all of our 150 reviews to find your perfect course – and don't miss our 'To Avoid' reviews! All for an irresistible 99p trial!

Indeed, this is not fiction: some private universities in the US have had lawsuits filed against them for making advertising claims that students felt were misleading, a trend which is now appearing in the UK (read more about this in the next chapter). To return to the scenario above; surveys are now a significant undertaking to inform customer choice. One survey in the US (Princeton Review 2014) surveys a wide range of customer experience (including the aspects mentioned in the scenario above, such as the quality of campus food and sportiness of classmates). In the UK, the National Student Survey which has now generated over 2 million responses between 2005 and 2013 (HEFCE 2014), focuses on teaching and learning experiences for enhancement purposes. Examples of these types of survey are outlined in the table below (Fig. 3.1).

The head of *Which? University* captures what seems to be the importance of surveys in such modern times, and in so doing reflects a Žižekian point about how expectations are generated by understanding higher education as a product. Jenni Allen says "With increased tuition fees, it's never been more important for prospective students to weigh up all the options and make sure they make the *right choice for them*" (Huffington Post 2013, emphasis added). This is, of course, the prime reason why the funding body for higher education (HEFCE) invented

Survey	Focus	Responses
National Student Survey (UK)	Measuring undergraduate student experience of learning and teaching.	**320,000+** (in 2014)
Princeton Review (US)	Measuring a wide range of features about the student experience.	**130,000** (in 2014)
Postgraduate Taught Experience Survey (UK)	Measuring the experience of taught postgraduate students in relation to learning, teaching and other aspects of their courses to enhance their experience.	**67,000+** (in 2014)
Postgraduate Research Experience Survey (UK)	Measuring the experience of postgraduate research students in relation to their teaching and learning, supervision and wider research environment, in order to enhance their experience.	**48,000+** (in 2013)
UK Engagement Survey	Measuring undergraduate student engagement to enhance learning and teaching.	**25,000+** (in 2014)
Which? (UK)	Measuring the student experience in order to enable potential students to "find the best one for you".	**16,000+** (in 2014)

Fig. 3.1 Survey of surveys (*Sources* HEFCE 2015b, c, d, e; Which? 2015; Princeton Review 2014)

Unistats, which collates and presents Key Information Sets (KIS). HEFCE describes KIS as containing:

> the items of information that prospective *students have identified as most important to inform their decisions*… All institutions also make this information available via a small snippet of content or 'widget' through the course pages on their web-sites. This is the first time this kind of data has been brought together in this way, *providing information to students in a format that is useful to them, in the places they want to find it.* (HEFCE 2013, emphasis added)

This comparative information is now extremely detailed in the UK and collates data from the Higher Education Statistics Agency, the Skills Funding Agency, educational establishments and the National Student Survey. With governmental mandate, students now have a right to access, through a 'widget', information such as:

- Student satisfaction from the National Student Survey
- Student destinations on finishing their course from the Destinations of Leavers from Higher Education survey
- How the course is taught and study patterns
- How the course is assessed
- Course accreditation
- Course costs (such as tuition fees and accommodation) (HEFCE 2015a).

Taking a Žižekian glance at this, is it not the case that the KIS of higher education is the *KeyFacts*® statement that the Financial Conduct Authority requires of all financial products sold in the UK? These 'key facts' are essentially the 'key information sets' of a loan, a bank account, pet insurance, dental care and so on. What is this telling us about how we understand education? From the sketch above, we might say that higher education in contemporary capitalist society, as well as establishments to give birth and to provide elderly care, is being understood in the same way as other commodities we have in our kitchens, or in our wallets or purses. Žižek argues that this is filtering through to all aspects of life, including the commodification of people (e.g. human trafficking, prostitution) and even religion (e.g. the authors have seen a local church with a large advertisement outside exclaiming *"Church: For Hire!"*) (Žižek 2014).

Other education scholars agree with this diagnosis. Miller (2010), for example, argues that when commodified as a product, higher education is bought for *credentials* to differentiate the buyer to enable them to compete in a job market, for *skills* in order to enter and participate a professional space, or simply to fulfil a wider expectation that they should *consume* higher education. Though tackling the same issue from a different perspective, Brown and Carasso (2013) demonstrate how market mechanisms are shaping the industrial structures of higher education, and specifically frame commodification in terms of how 'the student' is being understood as 'the consumer'.

But what about school education—does that escape? No—in many ways it has even led the way. Is it not the very same phenomenon we are seeing in school performance tables which are designed to enable prospective customers (parents) choose the 'perfect' school? Here, school education can be measured in terms of human development represented as qualification outcome achievement or 'value-added' (itself a commercial construct)—and can be filtered by search criteria such as small/large cohort size or gender mix (e.g. Education Advisors 2014). Does it not surprise us that there are now around 400 variables in which schools are measured to aid choice (see, for example, Department for Education 2015; Harrison 2014)?

Scholars argue that we have known about this trend to conceive of education at all levels in terms of economic utility for some time (Pring and Pollard 2011), but the Žižekian point here is that these recent moves (e.g. KIS in 2012) are a sign of how such trends are deepening. For Žižek, this is a consequence of how contemporary capitalist society embeds its reach into how we think and act: he argues that as we participate in all aspects of our life, we draw upon the Symbolic realm to make sense of what we are doing and who we are. In this Symbolic Order, we get clues, rules or points of reference as to how to subjectively make sense of our reality:

> There are the rules (and meanings) that I follow blindly, out of custom, but of which, upon reflection, I can become at least partially aware (such as common grammatical rules), and there are rules that I follow, meanings that haunt me, unbeknownst to me (such as unconscious prohibitions). Then there are rules and meanings I am aware of, but have to act on the outside as if I am not aware of them… which one passes over in silence in order to maintain the proper appearances. The symbolic space acts like a standard against which I can measure myself. (Žižek 2006, p. 9)

We *need* this Symbolic Order precisely because we cannot access the raw and overwhelming reality of what is 'underneath' the language we use to try to portray it. Here, Žižek agrees with Lacan (2006) and Foucault (1997) that it is impossible to access a reality 'underneath' social constructions, and dismisses Habermas's (1976) idea of trying to resolve how a society 'distorts' reality through its use of language. Žižek joins Lacau and Mouffee (1985) in their idea that there is no 'necessary relationship' between that which is being *signified*, and that which is used to *signify*. Rather, we choose from "a multitude of floating signifiers" which help us 'fix' a particular signification, providing a "quilt" or fixing effect to grasp the reality we are seeking to portray (Žižek 1989, p. 95).

Žižek gives the example of how a patient in a hospital bed is represented by the charts at the end of their bed; they are 'captured' through a display of temperature, blood pressure, medications and so on (Žižek 1998). The display (the signifier) represents the patient (being signified), within meaningful boxes or statistics; meaningful according to the body of medical knowledge, and the framings that construct it in this way. The story being told is not of the total reality of the person, but a whole that is determined to be meaningful by the medical world—or more specifically, by the constructs within medical knowledge. As such, representations are always acting from a partial perspective, never unbiased, never value-free, and never 'undistorted', but because they are operating out of awareness, they appear 'as if' this is how the world actually is.

In the case of education, we might use the terms 'pupil' or 'student' to represent the people we engage with in our practice every day, but if we did not have these, what are we referring to? We might alternatively use the term 'learner' or 'learning partner' to represent, but without *these* terms, what and who are we trying to portray? In the same way, and as we see above, we might also use the terms 'customer' or 'consumer', and even 'client' or 'partner', but if we didn't use these terms, what and who are we trying to portray? Importantly, although signifiers are 'violent' simplifications (Žižek 2008) of a reality we cannot fully access, they help us grasp the world we find ourselves in. And it is important that we desperately want these signifiers to fill the no-thing-ness, 'lack' or 'void' our subjectivity is built on (also see Sartre 1966). This is why Žižek refers to a kind of 'forced choice' between *some*-thing and *no*-thing, but which can only be known *after* entering the Symbolic realm (Žižek 2002, p. 69).

Signifiers are never neutral representations, but can be powerful structuring devices of themselves: "language does not simply name a reality which pre-exists it, but rather *produces* the concept of reality through the system of differences which *is* language" (Easthope and McGowan 1992, p. 68). As such, these representations embody the types of rules that Žižek refers to above, or what he also refers to as a 'Big Other', a "social repository of collected and projected beliefs, which we all relate to and reply upon" (Taylor 2010, p. 73). To return to the question above, if we did not use the words 'student', 'learner' or 'customer', we could of course say 'a mass of skin, bone and flesh'—but even this, though vulgar, is a representation from a particular angle, that is, a pseudo-biological angle. The point is that we *need* constructions to grasp what we are referring to and that each one embodies a particular way of seeing a particular dimension of what we are trying to grasp.

For Žižek, this is what we can now see across all dimensions of society, and is presented in the first part of this chapter: is this not vividly presented in the stories painted above about how education is represented and constructed in product rankings and reviews for prospective customers? Is this not a story of how a higher education establishment can be understood by potential customers by measures of teaching quality, research quality, quality of parties and amounts of alcohol consumed? This is a situation which is probably not surprising given the increasing trend towards the commodification of education in the UK and elsewhere, alongside the privatisation and marketisation of multiple educational sectors: from the introduction of academies which have to seek their own funding sources, through to higher education, which in the UK charges up to £9,000 per annum undergraduate tuition at the time of writing.

Within higher education, this trend is clear and prominent in recent policy directions. For example, the Leitch Review (2006) argued that attuning and servicing the demands of employers better would lead to "higher productivity, the creation of wealth and social justice" and that without it, "we would condemn ourselves to a lingering decline in competitiveness, diminishing economic growth and a bleaker future for all" (Leitch Review 2006, p. 1). This has echoed ever since, with the idea that flexibility is crucial for "the nation's strength in the global knowledge based economy" (Department for Business Innovation and Skills 2009, p. 15) (also see Department for Business Innovation and Skills 2009, 2010; Department for Innovation Universities and Skills 2008a, b; HEFCE 2010, 2011).

Some even argue that this 'three leg' model of higher education (where commercial income generation joins the pillars of teaching and research), is now obsolete and that the commercial expectation is no longer a discrete set of activity, but integral to higher education life (Barnett 2003, 2011; Brown and Carasso 2013; Collini 2012). Indeed, Taylor (2010) highlights how over time, the responsibility of universities within the UK Government has shifted from a 'Department of Education' to, more recently, a 'Department for Business, Innovation and Skills'; cutting out 'education' to emphasise commerce. England's 80 % teaching budget cuts in 2011 exemplifies this drive further, but also emphasises and deepens this drive, in the sense that now, university income is largely dependent on individual educational purchasers in the marketplace, and educational professionals have a direct role in serving the customer in satisfying that demand.

(Ant)Agonising Bureaucracy

When we wear Žižekian glasses, we are also exposed to possible antagonisms or contradictions as a way of understanding the ways in which such Symbolic grips hold us (inspired by Marx and Hegel). This will be discussed in more detail later on, but let us raise an alternative view of education which we might be aware of, and frustrate us, in our daily practice. And it links precisely to the question: if education is being understood in the business-oriented ways sketched out above, and has been for such a long time, then why is education supposedly failing to meet the needs of our global economy, and specifically the needs of business organisations within it? For example, in the context of school education, governmental advisory groups use surveys to help measure our performance globally:

> ...surveys by employers and higher education institutions in the UK have suggested that students are not as well prepared as they should be by age 18 for the transition from secondary education to employment and/or to university. Concomitantly, international surveys of educational attainment in different countries in core competences such as reading and mathematics suggest that our performance is standing still while other countries, with fast growing economies, are moving forward to meet the educational needs in a fast changing world. (Anderson 2014, p. 6)

Why might this contradiction happen? Within the context of higher education, there is a joke never shared which helps explore this further: a business executive walks into a university and asks "what do I have to do to get *a* credit round here?". The comedic value (if there is one) is that this innocently naïve question actually does appear in practice, but is an utterly nonsensical question for those immersed *in* the world of the bureaucracy of academe: credits in the UK are typically understood in terms of in bigger chunks, such as 10, 15 or 20 credits—and not as a single credit as such (of course, this joke has even less value cross borders, such as in the US where it is quite possible and legitimate to study a course the size of a credit or three). Nonetheless, the joke serves the purpose of illuminating the disconnect between alternative, even oppositional, understandings of education—one in terms of a demand for some-thing (a credit) that does not necessarily exist in that form (usually 10, 15 or 20 credits). In other words, it provides a way of illustrating alternative ways of drawing from the Symbolic realm, with an alternative language set and associated set of values and beliefs.

This disconnect in language between business and higher education establishments has been widely reported as a source of frustration and friction (see, for example, Bolden et al. 2009, 2010; CBI 2008, 2009; Cooper et al. 2008; Wedgewood 2008). For some, higher education is "incomprehensible" (McDonald 2009; Cooper et al. 2008), and that bureaucratic processes and culture are slow and problematic (Cooper et al. 2008). Other research has even identified the same issues *within* a university (Poole 2010). In this version of higher education, rather than being painted as a product to be bought, higher education is painted as a bureaucratic system with boxes to fill; boxes for the number of academic credits, boxes for the academic level, boxes for learning outcomes, boxes for grades, boxes for passes/fails, boxes for assessment items, boxes for attendance, boxes for amount paid, and so on (Wall 2013).

In other words, education is painted as a highly structured framework, a device of a bureaucrat monitoring consistency and comparability. These are not managed by one single body, but governed and policed by multiple and powerful watchdogs, underpinned by a particular, but common, way of thinking about what education is. Such academic frameworks are sublime in contemporary society and transcend educational sector: in the UK we have National Occupational Standards (NOS), have the National Qualifications Framework (NQF), the Qualifications and Credit Framework (QCF) and the Framework for Higher Education Qualifications (FHEQ), not to mention the National Curriculum (Brown and McNamara 2011; Brown et al. 2006) and other professional and awarding bodies (Robson 2006). Outside of the UK, we have the European Credit Transfer (and accumulation) System (ECTS) across Europe, Hong Kong has its Hong Kong Qualifications Framework (HKQF), Australia has its Australian Qualifications Framework (AQF) and Singapore has its Workforce Skills Qualifications (WSQ) framework. Now, in the US, we have The Global Learning Qualifications Framework (GLQF) (see Travers and McQuigge 2013).

The latter of these, the GLQF, epitomises the idea of understanding education in terms of highly structured units: it is a framework of frameworks from 90 countries, and was created to asses higher education level learning 'regardless of where, when or how it was acquired'—whether that be from formally accredited educational establishments, informal training at work, or whether it is from Open Educational Resources (OERs) or Massive Open Online Courses (MOOCs) (Empire State College 2015). The list of abbreviations at the front of this book encapsulates how education is understood when viewed from a bureaucratic perspective, but is no match for the lists offered by the California Department of Education which lists over 300 terms, the New York State Department for Education's list of over 450 terms (NY State Education Department 2015), or even the New South Wales' Department of Education and Communities list which defines over 500 terms (NSW Government 2015). The University of Cambridge's handbook of educational abbreviations and terms perhaps beats them all, with abbreviations spanning over 120 pages (Hickman 2013). It is not surprising that there are such challenges in understanding the language of education.

So why do these constructions and associated images matter to Žižek? How do these social constructions of education filter through to how people act within educational settings? For Žižek, these images have literally dramatic consequences, and implicate how we make sense of and therefore engage with education. Teachers, students, what education is and does, as well as others engaged in the exchange of the educational product are all impacted in not so obvious ways. Now, how such constructions propel and compel us is the focus of the next chapter.

References

Anderson, R. (2014). *Careers 2020: Making education work—A report from an independent advisory group chaired by Professor Sir Roy Anderson*. London: Pearson.

Barnett, R. (2003). *Beyond all reason: Living with ideology in the university*. London: Society for Research into Higher Education.

Barnett, R. (2011). The coming of the ecological university. *Oxford Review of Education, 37*(4), 439–455.

Bolden, R., Connor, H., Duquemin, A., Hirsh, W., & Petrov, G. (2009). *Employer engagement with higher education: Defining, sustaining, and supporting higher skills provision*. London: Department for Innovation, Universities and Skills.

Bolden, R., Hirsh, W., Connor, H., Petrov, G., & Duquemin, A. (2010). *Strategies for effective HE-employer engagement*. London: Department for Innovation, Universities and Skills.

Brown, R., & Carasso, H. (2013). *Everything for sale? The marketisation of higher education*. London: Society for Research into Higher Education.

Brown, T., Atkinson, D., & England, J. (2006). *Regulative discourses in education: A Lacanian perspective*. London: Peter Lang publishers.

Brown, T., & McNamara, O. (2011). *Becoming a mathematics teacher: Identity and identifications*. Dordrecht: Springer.

CBI. (2008). *Stepping higher: Workforce development through employer-higher education partnership*. London: Confederation of British Industry.

CBI. (2009). *Stronger together: Businesses and universities in turbulent times*. London: Department for Business, Innovation and Skills.

Collini, S. (2012). *What are universities for*? London: Penguin.

Cooper, C., Mackinnon, I., & Garside, P. (2008). *Employer engagement research report 29*. Wath-upon-Dearne: Sector Skills Development Agency.

Department for Business Innovation and Skills. (2009). *Higher ambitions: The future of universities in a knowledge economy*. London: Department for Business, Innovation and Skills.

Department for Business Innovation and Skills. (2010). *Securing a sustainable future for higher education: An independent review of higher education funding and student finance*. London: Department for Business, Innovation and Skills.

Department for Education. (2015). *School performance tables*. Retrieved January 26, 2015, from http://www.education.gov.uk/schools/performance/.

Department for Innovation Universities and Skills. (2008a). *The debate on the future of higher education*. Retrieved March 14, 2015, from http://webarchive.nationalarchives.gov.uk/20090902220721/; http://www.dius.gov.uk/higher_education/shape_and_structure/he_debate.

Department for Innovation Universities and Skills. (2008b). *Higher education at work: The future of universities in a knowledge economy*. London: Department for Innovation, Universities and Skills.

Easthope, A., & McGowan, K. (1992). *A critical and cultural theory reader*. Buckingham: Open University Press.

Education Advisors. (2014). *Best schools ranking*. Retrieved January 26, 2015, from http://www.best-schools.co.uk/.

Empire State College. (2015). *The global learning qualifications framework*. Retrieved March 15, 2015, from http://www.esc.edu/suny-real/global-learning-qualifications-framework/.

Foucault, M. (1997). *Ethics*. London: Penguin.

Habermas, J. (1976). Systematically distorted communication. In: P. Connerton (Ed.), *Critical Sociology*. Harmondsworth: Penguin.

Harrison, A. (2014). BBC News—School league tables: Many ways to measure schools. *BBC News*. Retrieved March 14, 2015, from http://www.bbc.com/news/education-25868976.

HEFCE. (2010). *The higher education workforce framework 2010*. Retrieved March 14, 2015, from http://www.hefce.ac.uk/pubs/hefce/2010/10_05/.

HEFCE. (2011). *Engaging employers with higher education: HEFCE strategy to support links between higher education and employers on skills and lifelong learning*. Retrieved March 14, 2015, from http://www.hefce.ac.uk/econsoc/employer/.

HEFCE. (2013). *Unistats and key information sets*. Retrieved February 13, 2015, from http://www.hefce.ac.uk/whatwedo/lt/publicinfo/kis/.

HEFCE. (2014). *UK review of the provision of information about higher education: National student survey results and trends analysis 2005–2013*. Retrieved March 14, 2015, from https://www.hefce.ac.uk/media/hefce/content/pubs/2014/201413/HEFCE2014_13%20-%20corrected%2012%20December%202014.pdf.

HEFCE. (2015a). *About unistats*. Retrieved February 17, 2015, from https://unistats.direct.gov.uk/find-out-more/about-unistats/.

HEFCE. (2015b). *National student survey*. Retrieved January 17, 2015, from https://www.hefce.ac.uk/whatwedo/lt/publicinfo/nss/.

HEFCE. (2015c). *Postgraduate research experience survey*. Retrieved January 17, 2015, from https://www.heacademy.ac.uk/consultancy-services/surveys/pres.

HEFCE. (2015d). *Postgraduate taught experience survey*. Retrieved January 17, 2015, from https://www.heacademy.ac.uk/consultancy-services/surveys/ptes.

HEFCE. (2015e). *United Kingdom engagement survey*. Retrieved January 17, 2015, https://www.heacademy.ac.uk/consultancy-services/surveys/ukes.

Hickman, R. (2013). *C.H.E.A.T Cambridge handbook of educational abbreviations & terms* (6th ed.). Cambridge: University of Cambridge.

Huffington Post. (2013). *The Huffington post—Best and worst universities in the UK ranked by Which? student survey*. Retrieved March 14, 2015, from http://www.huffingtonpost.co.uk/2013/09/11/best-worst-universities-in-the-uk_n_3904531.html.

Lacan, J. (2006). *Ecrits. The first complete edition in English translated by Bruce Fink*. New York: W. W. Norton.

Lacau, E., & Mouffee, C. (1985). *Hegemony and socialist strategy*. London: Verso.

Leitch Review. (2006). *The Leitch review of skills: Prosperity for all in the global economy—world class skills*. Norwich: HMSO.

McDonald, K. (2009). *A report on the relevance of language barriers to work based learning/employer engagement*. York: Higher Education Academy.

Miller, B. (2010). Skills for sale: What is being commodified in higher education? *Journal of Further and Higher Education, 34*(2), 199–206.

NSW Goverment. (2015). *NSW education and communities—A-Z acronyms and abbreviations*. Retrieved March 15, 2015, from http://www.dec.nsw.gov.au/about-us/information-access/a-z-of-acronyms-and-abbreviation.

NY State Education Department. (2015). *New York State education department—acronyms*. Retrieved March 15, 2015 from http://www.nysed.gov/about/acronyms.

Poole, B. (2010). Quality, semantics and the two cultures. *Quality Assurance in Education, 18*(1), 6–18.

Review, Princeton. (2014). *The best 379 colleges: 2015 edition*. Natick MA: The Princeton Review Education IP Holdings LLC.

Pring, R., & Pollard, A. (2011). *Education for all: Evidence from the past, principles for the future*. London: The ESRC Teaching & Learning Research Programme.

Robson, J. (2006). *Teacher professionalism in further and Higher Education*. Abingdon: Routledge.

Sartre, J. P. (1966). *Being and nothingness*. New York: Simon & Schuster.

Taylor, P. (2010). *Žižek and the Media*. Cambridge: Polity Press.

Travers, N. L., & McQuigge, A. (2013). The global learning qualifications framework. *PLA Inside Out, 2*(1).

Wall, T. (2013). *Professional identities and commodification in higher education*. Unpublished Doctoral Thesis, Manchester Metropolitan University, Manchester.

Wedgewood, M. (2008). *Higher Education for the workforce—Barriers and facilitators to employer engagement*. London: Department for Innovation, Universities and Skills.

Which? (2015). *Which? university*. Retrieved January 17, 2015, from http://university.which.co.uk/.

Žižek, S. (1989). *The sublime object of ideology*. London: Verso.

Žižek, S. (1998). Four discourses. Four subjects. In S. Žižek (ed.) *Cogito and the unconscious*. Durham, NC: Duke University.

Žižek, S. (2002). *Enjoy your symptom! Jacques Lacan in hollywood and out* (2nd ed.). London: Routledge.

Žižek, S. (2006). *The parallax view*. Cambridge, MA: MIT Press.

Žižek, S. (2008). *Violence*. London: Profile.

Žižek, S. (2013). *Denial: The liberal utopia*. Retrieved January 17, 2015, from http://www.lacan.com/essays/?page_id=397.

Žižek, S. (2014). *Event*. London: Penguin.

Chapter 4
Mobilising 'Customer *as* King'

Abstract Where do we start if we should wish to change the demands students (the customer) place on their teachers (their service provider)? For Žižek, the problem is that this is a near impossible task, because contemporary capitalism is so entrenched in our everyday lives. The Symbolic realm does not belong to one educational establishment or educational sector, but is pervasive across society: governing frameworks shape all aspects of educational life, from institutional policies, to disciplinary knowledge structures, through to the way marking sheets of educational assessments are laid out. This far-reaching Symbolic realm not only guides us in how we understand education, but contains other seeds of why is it so difficult to achieve educational reform which goes beyond tinkering around the edges of curriculum re-design or educational policy. Žižek alerts us to how the Symbolic infects our unconscious motivations to create images of ourselves, thereby shaping how we think we should act. Moreover, something always escapes capture by the Symbolic, and because this fragmentation is traumatic, we are propelled and mobilised in ways towards acting in accordance with a more coherent and unified self-image. This spurs us to continually attempt to strive to be coherent as a 'customer demanding good customer service' or a 'teacher, imparting knowledge'. Žižek suggests that, together, these provide a powerful motivational mechanism towards enacting and re-enacting out the same behaviours, which are near impossible to change unless we challenge the very grounds, including language, on which we engage.

Keywords Desire · Drive · Unconscious · The imaginary · Self-image · Motivation

© The Author(s) 2015
T. Wall and D. Perrin, *Slavoj Žižek*,
SpringerBriefs on Key Thinkers in Education,
DOI 10.1007/978-3-319-21242-5_4

Expectation, Expectation, Expectation

Depending on the circles you frequent, you may have heard about the Master of Business Administration award, the MBA, and how it might be seen as a qualification that attracts a premium. Should you seek a Harvard University MBA, the "MBA Class of 2016 Student Budget" for a single person is shown in the table below (Harvard Business School 2015), and cost around US \$95,000 (which is approximately GB £62,000, or EU €83,000). To put that into perspective at the time of writing, that could buy a spacious 4 bedroom apartment in Abu Dhabi, buy three brand new A Class Mercedes-Benz cars in the UK, pay for the tuition of almost two children to boarding prep-school in Switzerland, or buy over 2,500 copies of the *20th Anniversary Edition* of the book *The McDonaldization of Society* (Ritzner 2012)—or of course, over 12,000 Big Mac meals. Another perspective is that the fees for one Harvard MBA student would equate to the annual allowance the UK government would give to 20 people who need extra personal support in their homes (Age UK 2015).

Is it a surprise then to hear stories about a whole cohort of MBA students complaining to their business school Dean when the position of their MBA slips in global rankings? For Žižek, this is a story about how certain expectations are activated when we engage in the Symbolic realm in particular ways. These expectations do not only relate to what is expected from education, but also ourselves as participants in that educational activity. In other words, the total subjective landscape of our engagement is tainted by the Symbolic realm in which we engage: if we pay US \$95,000, it taints what we think we are paying for as well as what we think about those involved in the situation. In this case, that is, we are set up as customer and provider. This explains how when these expectations are not met, we feel disgruntled and disappointed, and we may even wish we had 'invested' our hard earned money on 12,000 Big Macs meals rather than the MBA (Fig. 4.1).

The expectations activated for these high-fee-paying MBA students are not unique to them; Žižek suggests that they are a symptom of how deeply connected we are to contemporary capitalism. Žižek argues that much of this is a consequence of today's global capitalism which grips us even at the individual level to reconceptualise the individual as an 'entrepreneur-of-the-self' (Lazzarato 2012). Here, we live in circumstances which:

> extend the logic of market competition to all areas of social life so that… education… [is] perceived as investments made by the individuals in his or her capital. In this way, the worker is no longer conceived as labour power, but as personal capital making good or bad 'investment' decisions. (Žižek 2014, p. 42)

We do not have to look far to see how such expectations are alive across multiple educational systems. Within the context of higher education, the Office of the Independent Adjudicator for Higher Education (OIA) was established in 2004 to review and resolve student complaints that higher education establishments cannot resolve by themselves. In other words, it was set up to deal with students who do not feel that their expectations have been met. OIA data paints a similar picture to

Educational costs	Cost US $
Tuition	$58,875
Student health fee	$992
Student health insurance	$2,366
Program support fee (e.g. books)	$7,360
Room and utilities (9 months)	$11,544
Board, personal, other (9 months)	$13,963
Total	$95,100

Fig. 4.1 Example MBA Student Budget (*Source* Harvard Business School 2015)

the disgruntled MBA cohort above: by 2013, the OIA had received record numbers of complaints from students, after a year on year increase of 25 % (OIA 2013). During 2012, over 2,000 complaints were sent to the OIA in England and Wales alone (OIA 2013). By 2014, even though there was a slight decrease in the number of complaints, there had been an increase by two thirds in the amount of financial compensation the OIA has instructed universities to pay—that is, GBP £313,750 in compensation alone (OIA 2014). This amount is enough to pay for 5 people to attend the Harvard MBA. And is it surprising that the largest proportion (15 %) of the students complaining are from the business studies subject area (OIA 2014)? Is business education not one of the more direct instruments for instilling the values and beliefs important in contemporary capitalist society?

In what areas do students feel their expectations are not being met? In the OIA's latest case study (at the time of writing), a whole cohort of students complained about "the course publicity material, the course content and its academic quality, the quality of teaching staff and the lack of industry standard course materials" (see Case 86, OIA 2015). The OIA recommended each student was paid compensation. In another case, a student was awarded over GB £56,000 for fees and living expenses due to complaints against supervision and feedback. The student, however, demanded an *additional* GB £60,000 compensation in relation to "3 years' wasted effort, additional living expenses…, loss of earnings and damage to his reputation" (see Case 44, OIA 2015). Though these are single cases, it is possible to see glimpses into a variety of student expectations across the OIA's 86 published cases online, openly available to the public.

Of course, data from the OIA is only scratching the surface of this phenomenon of unmet expectation; these are only the cases that students do not feel have been fully resolved by the higher education establishment. In 2014, the BBC collated complaint data from 120 Freedom of Information requests sent to UK higher education institutions. The findings echoed that of the OIA: that complaints are at their highest, with around 20,000 student complaints per annum, and that the total paid out in compensation by universities as a result was more than GB £2 m since 2010 (Abrams 2014). In light of this, former UK's Universities Minister, David Willetts, revealed a Žižekian point about how these expectations have been activated:

> if there are more complaints because students are more aware of what they *should expect* of funding and are more *demanding*, then I think that's a good thing… When there's a fee of £9,000, the university is *obliged* to show what they're doing and *provide a decent service*. (Abrams 2014, emphasis added)

Indeed, yet another national survey supports these statements, which found drops in perceived 'value for money' since the introduction of fees, and found that students wanted their institution to prioritise spending on "increasing teaching hours: decreasing class sizes; better training for lecturers; and better learning facilities" (Soilemetzidis et al. 2014, p. 37). It is not surprising that the UK's higher education *sector* was referred by the then Office of Fair Trading to the new Competition and Markets Authority. Is it not a serious concern for a whole industry to be under scrutiny by the key consumer protection watchdog in the UK? The referral aims to *remind* the sector of its "responsibilities… under consumer protection law" and to identify "the best way to address these issues" (Competition and Markets Authority 2014). Notice the key framing here, given the context of education: Office of Fair *Trading*, and the *Competition* and *Markets* Authority. Bodies which are focused on *consumer* protection are now fully entrenched in education, working through and in the Symbolic of education as a commodified, saleable product.

But let us clarify that we are not making judgements about whether or not the students claims are valid; the precise Žižekian point that we are trying to make is that when we perceive and understand education in certain ways, we are implicated. When students are framed as purchasers of education, the student as customer expects a particular level of *customer service*. And the professional engaged in providing the service do not escape capture by the Symbolic: Žižek reminds us that the Symbolic taints every-thing it tries to capture. We can see evidence of this in Whitchurch's extensive, cross-nation empirical research (Whitchurch 2008a, b, 2009, 2010). She argues that roles previously demarked by professional spaces such as academic and non-academic (or administrative support) are merging, and that "blended professionals" are emerging. These are people who are involved in a wide range of tasks such as curricula design (previously a typical academic task) with 'client' or 'student experience' management (previously a typical non-academic or administrative support task). In the same way, Smith (2012) refers to this as the emergence of 'flexians', that is, people who are experiencing a larger and increasingly varied range of demands in their work.

Other scholars have also alluded to such shifts in how teachers understand their relationship with their students across educational sectors (Brown et al. 2006; Brown and McNamara 2011; Meakin and Wall 2013; Randle and Brady 1997; Robson 2006; Wall 2013). In their extensive and broad review, Pring and Pollard (2011) found that education is increasingly being understood in very narrow terms for economic utility, and is limiting the forms of learning and teaching across sectors. Brown and McNamara (2011) found the same within the context of mathematics education: forms of mathematics knowledge had been shaped by a wider drive towards forms which were readily testable within the school system. We will return to this again in the final chapter.

These trends also point to the work of other educational researchers with similar concerns to Žižek. Such scholars argue that there is an increase in the number of different belief systems at work within education which can make it difficult or near impossible to judge how to act on a daily basis (Barnett 2000, 2003, 2011; Rowland 2002). Here, professional life is not just a matter of "handling overwhelming data and theories *within* a given frame of reference", but rather a matter of "handling multiple frames of understanding... The fundamental frameworks by which we might understand the world are multiplying and are often in conflict" (Barnett 2000, p. 6). For example, Barnett (2003) refers to the frameworks of entrepreneurialism (as a drive towards exploiting new markets), quality assurance (as a drive for consistency and parity of units of education) and managerialism (as a drive for more efficient and effective use of resources). In such situations, contemporary educationalists need to be "willing to consider different understandings of their role" (Bolden et al. 2009, p. 36).

Wall's (2013) research provides multiple, contemporary examples of how educational professionals experience tensions in knowing how to act legitimately when faced with differing expectations. One example considers interactions of an academic with senior business executives studying on higher education programmes. On the one hand, there was a sensed expectation to deliver an excellent service with the business executives, in terms of engaging them and enabling them to progress through their programme. On the other hand, there was a felt expectation to adhere to academic convention, such as referencing according to the Harvard Referencing Style. In circumstances where the senior executive did not apply the correct referencing style in their academic writing, the educational professional experienced tension from encountering the two expectations: *is it appropriate to continually request that the learner applies correct academic referencing conventions to pass a module?* The tension revolves around sensing a need to get the senior executive to reference properly, *against* a feeling that doing so would not be valuable to the senior executive in their work, that is, it would not be providing an excellent service.

How might the tensions of having to deal with competing demands be playing out on a wider scale, within the wider trend towards the marketisation across educational sectors? By this, we do not mean how many teachers become anxious about how to approach a senior executive about how to reference Frank Furedi's *Wasted! Why Education isn't Educating*. Rather, what is the cumulative effect of such pressures in our work? A University and College Union (UCU) survey of over 8,000 professionals in 2014 found that 85 % of respondents in higher education had experienced "unacceptable" levels of stress in their job—the figure was 93 % in the case of further education (UCU 2014). Moreover, 60 % of higher education respondents had experienced levels of psychological distress that would normally trigger some sort of intervention (according to Health and Safety Executive guidelines). The most common pressures related to work demands, change management, management support, relationships and role clarity (UCU 2014). Similar research with 24,000 respondents the year before broadly reflected the same (Kinman and Wray 2013).

In terms of teaching in schools, the Health and Safety Executive found this to be the most stressful profession in the UK (Smith et al. 2000). More recently in 2012, the Guardian newspaper undertook its own research through Freedom of Information requests to 60 educational authorities (Ratcliffe 2012). It found teachers taking sick leave *as a result of stress* had increased by 10 % over the past 4 years. By 2013, the National Union of Teachers (NUT) was clearly concerned about this trend, and the possibility that 1 in 3 teachers take sick leave as a result of work-related stress, and released guidance on how to deal with it (NUT 2013). Here, a similar story to higher and further education professionals is painted: teachers are plagued by excessive workloads and working hours (exacerbated by multiple government 'initiatives'), poor pupil behaviour, the pressures of assessment targets and inspections, as well as conflict with managers or colleagues (NUT 2013). The NUT also warned teachers of the ways in which stress can materialise physically at work, largely reflecting the same in a higher education study (Sparkes 2007):

> headaches, raised blood pressure, infections, digestive disorders, heart disease or cancer; mental health symptoms such as withdrawal, poor concentration, anxiety, depression, insomnia, 'burn-out' and an increased risk of suicide; and behavioural consequences such as low self-esteem, increased drug or alcohol intake and deteriorating personal relationships leading to family, relationship or career problems. (NUT 2013, p. 2)

Alongside trends towards increasingly excessive demands placed on educational workers and how these can result such physically destructive consequences, there may (or may not) be hope. It may (or may not) be assuring to know that there is now an insurance company that specialises in covering the costs incurred by schools as a result of teacher absence. In true customer-centric fashion, the Schools Advisory Service (SAS) gives school managers a level of cover to match their specific needs and budgetary constraints:

> We provide a flexible, bespoke cover to each and every school. You can tailor make your policy by choosing the daily benefit amount you would like to receive from £70 to £250 per day, the number of days you would like to wait before receiving payment from 0 to 30 days. You can also choose whether you would like to include maternity cover, and if you would this can be from £750 to £5,000. (SAS 2015)

So the Žižekian point is that the buy-into this Symbolic is widespread: the student buys into it, educational professionals buy into it, government ministers buy into it, and so do others who are within the system (including the suppliers of specialist insurance companies that have been set up to manage the consequences of the pressures of that very system). To illustrate the point, even the OIA has procedures for *dealing with complaints* for its organisational remit of *dealing with complaints*, and is driven to serve its customers better: it wants to reduce the "the *unit cost* of closing complaints" (which was £1,661 in 2013), to close 75 % of cases within 6 months (OIA 2014), and make improvements "around the clarity, tone and timeliness of communications" (OIA 2014). This echoes the public report by leaders at the University of California which details how they have responded to the increasing marketisation of higher education over the past two decades, and how they have, as a result, reduced the cost of education to the lowest in 20 years (University of California 2015). In other words, the Symbolic deeply entrenches whole educational systems.

Seeing Kings and Subjects in the Mirror

These stories are glimpses into the consequences of what happens when we call upon the Symbolic realm as we live our lives in and out of educational settings. To begin to explain what Žižek thinks is happening in these stories, we will do as he does and refer to interpellation (Althusser 2001), but do so only as a partial explanation as we will soon see. Imagine you are walking along when all of a sudden someone shouts 'hey you there!' (or whistles at you). You turn around, thinking that it is for you. The point is that precisely because you have turned around, you have been *hailed*, or you have *become* the addressee. Whether you believe it, suspect it or know it, the hail has already implicated your practice. It is the same when a teacher is trying to manage a rowdy pair of students at the back of a classroom: when a teacher exclaims 'stop!', even the students quietly and diligently working on the set task look up, wondering if it *might* apply to them. Through their action, they have been implicated or hailed by the call. What about when a school's head teacher sends out an email to all of their teachers requesting them to reduce the amount of photocopying? As soon as a teacher thinks 'are they referring to me?', they have been hailed, called and implicated, whether it applies to them or not.

For Žižek, this is how we are implicated when we engage with the Symbolic: as soon as we say 'customer' or 'king', we have *already* activated particular expectations of what that thing is and how we should relate to it. But it is insufficient to say that we simply put on a tainted *lens* which taints what we can *see*, but rather, and in addition, the *looker* is also tainted. By this we mean that when we use language, the Symbolic "encapsulates the [imaginary] individual looking out to a fantasy world filtered through the ideological framings brought to it" (Brown et al. 2006, p. 39). Here, images of self are shaped "within the terms which the laws of language allow" (Easthope and McGowan 1992, p. 68). This is succinctly illustrated when Raechel Mattey, the National Union of Students' Vice President (Union Development) says "Students do *see* themselves more as consumers… They want the best possible degree they can get" (Abrams 2014, emphasis added).

This is the realm of the Imaginary, where the Symbolic shapes images of who we are and therefore expectations of how we think we should act, including how people relate to the others and things around them. Žižek illustrates this with

Hegel's observation "No man is a hero to his valet". Here, this is not because "the man is not a hero, but because the valet is a valet, whose dealings are with the man, not as a hero, but as one who eats, drinks, and wears clothes" (Hegel cited in Žižek 2000, p. 48). Or in the case of being a 'king' and the king's 'subjects':

> 'Being-a-king' is an effect of the network of social relations between a 'king' and his 'subjects'; but… to the participants of this social bond, the relationship appears necessarily in an inverse form: they think that they are subjects giving the king royal treatment because the king is already in himself, outside the relationship to his subjects, a king; as if the determination of 'being-a-king' were a 'natural' property of the person of a king. (Žižek 1994, p. 309)

In other words, a king is treated as such because the expectations of what it means to act like a king, to act like a subject, and how the two should interact, are already in place, shaping all involved. And does this not beautifully echo the stories presented in this chapter? Do the stories in this chapter not suggest that we could perhaps tweak Raechel Mattey's statement to capture how people relate in contemporary higher education: '*students see themselves as Kings, when they look in the mirror*' and perhaps add '*teachers see themselves as Subjects, when they look in the mirror*'? In a similar vein, Harrison (2012) found that in the context of indigenous education in Australia, teachers in his study were "teaching what *they* want Aboriginal people to be" (Harrison 2012, p. 6, emphasis added) rather than allowing or enabling the students to discover alternative representations.

These images, with all they contain, are crucial: we desperately need them to avoid the psychic trauma of lack or no-thing-ness (Žižek 2002, p. 69), but also to deal with the psychic overwhelm of 'brute' reality (Žižek 2009). This is why Žižek says that "to achieve self-identity, the subject must identify himself with the imaginary other, he must alienate himself—put his identity outside himself, so to speak, into the image of his double" (Žižek 1989, p. 116). The point Žižek is making here is analogous with the moment we look into a mirror and say 'that's me'. Here, we are mis-recognising the mirror image as 'me', that is, we are acting 'as if' there is a single, unified image of self. The mirror, however, can only ever provide 'violently' simplified, and therefore fictional, versions of self (Žižek 2008). Our need for order and coherence of self is so strong that painful deviances from a coherent image are bracketed out, to the favour of the unified image (Žižek 2009). So to return to the notion of interpellation, Žižek might suggest that it is not that we are interpellate (as something done to us), but rather we interpellate ourselves towards the pleasure of coherence and the unity of self.

However, for Žižek, that which escapes capture by the Symbolic, or in the gaze of the mirror, propels us forward through our unconscious desires and drives (Žižek 2006). As Žižek claims, "we cannot ever acquire a complete, all-encompassing sense of reality—some part of it must be affected by the "loss of reality", deprived of the character of true reality" (Žižek 2001, p. 66). Žižek here is referring precisely to the Lacanian Real, a dimension which is never fully knowable as it is "that which resists… all symbolisation" (Lacan, quoted in Critchley 2008, p. 63). Importantly, that which escapes capture holds the source of what compels and propels us, or as

Žižek explains, it is the "surplus of the Real over every symbolization that functions as the object-cause of desire" (Žižek 1989, p. xxv). He says:

> the last support of the ideological effect (of the way an ideological network of signifiers "holds" us) is the... kernel of enjoyment. In ideology, "all is not ideological (that is, ideological meaning)", but it is this very surplus which is the last support of ideology. (Žižek 1989, p. 140)

How does it operate in this way? That which escapes capture in the Symbolic does this by creating a painful discomfort through a sense of lack, or something missing, thereby propelling into a constant search for some-thing—desire—a kind of 'wish' for some-thing (Lacan 1981; Žižek 1989). Yet this seeking provides us with an "enjoyment" for as long as this lack is experienced (Žižek 1994, p. 330). Specifically, this creates a situation of gaining pleasure from repetitive loops of trying to fully capture (through the Symbolic) but failing (something always escapes). And a specific form of desire is when we no longer even need to capture that which escapes—drive (Žižek 2006)—where we "get caught into a closed, self propelling loop of repeating the same gesture and finding satisfaction in it" (Žižek 2006, p. 63). Within education, this often appears when we successfully work within the parameters of completing a proforma or template, or regulative frameworks (Brown 2008).

This all helps to explain how significant the Symbolic images illustrated in this book so far are within contemporary education: they provide the coordinates of not only what education is, but also how the people involved in it make sense of themselves, and therefore how they feel they should act within daily settings. These simplified versions, caught by the Symbolic, are so powerful in the way they shape what and how we see, and therefore how we engage in our educational settings, which is why Žižek goes as far as saying that "things (commodities) themselves believe in [our] place" (Žižek 1989, p. 31). Yet for Žižek, this is only part of the story that explains why it is so difficult to effect changes within contemporary education. The next chapter now picks up more of the story.

References

Abrams, F. (2014). *BBC News—University complaints by students top 20,000*. Retrieved March 14, 2015, from http://www.bbc.co.uk/news/education-27640303.

Age UK. (2015). *Attendance allowance*. Retrieved February 13, 2015, from http://www.ageuk.org.uk/money-matters/claiming-benefits/attendance-allowance/what-is-attendance-allowance/.

Althusser, L. (2001). *Lenin and philosophy, and other essays*. New York: Monthly Review Press.

Barnett, R. (2000). *Realizing the university in an age of supercomplexity*. Buckingham: Open University/Society for Research into Higher Education.

Barnett, R. (2003). *Beyond all reason: Living with ideology in the university*. London: Society for Research into Higher Education.

Barnett, R. (2011). The coming of the ecological university. *Oxford Review of Education, 37*(4), 439–455.

Bolden, R., Connor, H., Duquemin, A., Hirsh, W., & Petrov, G. (2009). *Employer engagement with higher education: Defining, sustaining, and supporting higher skills provision.* London: Department for Innovation, Universities and Skills.

Brown, T. (2008). Desire and drive in researcher subjectivity: The broken mirror of Lacan. *Qualitative Inquiry, 14*(2), 402–423.

Brown, T., Atkinson, D., & England, J. (2006). *Regulative discourses in education: A Lacanian perspective.* London: Peter Lang Publishers.

Brown, T., & McNamara, O. (2011). *Becoming a mathematics teacher: Identity and identifications.* Dordrecht: Springer.

Competition and Markets Authority. (2014). *Higher education: Consumer protection review.* Retrieved February 17, 2015, from https://www.gov.uk/cma-cases/consumer-protection-review-of-higher-education-in-england.

Critchley, S. (2008). *Infinitely demanding: Ethics of commitment, politics of resistance.* London: Verso.

Easthope, A., & McGowan, K. (1992). *A critical and cultural theory reader.* Buckingham: Open University Press.

Harrison, N. (2012). Aborigines of the imaginary: Applying Lacan to aboriginal education. *Asia-Pacific Journal of Teacher Education, 40*(1), 5–14.

Harvard Business School. (2015). *Cost summary.* Retrieved February 13, 2015 from http://www.hbs.edu/mba/financial-aid/Pages/cost-summary.aspx.

Kinman, G., & Wray, S. (2013). *Higher stress: A survey of stress and well-being among staff in higher education.* London: The University and College Union.

Lacan, J. (1981). *Le Seminaire III - Les Psychoses.* Paris: Seuil.

Lazzarato, M. (2012). *The making of the indebted man: Essay on the neoliberal condition.* Amsterdam: Semiotext.

Meakin, D., & Wall, T. (2013). Co-delivered work based learning: Contested ownership and responsibility. *Higher Education, Skills & Work Based Learning, 3*(1), 73–81.

NUT. (2013). *Teacher stress: NUT guidance to divisions and associations.* London: The National Union of Teachers.

OIA. (2013). *OIA annual report 2012.* Reading: Office of the Independent Adjudicator for Higher Education.

OIA. (2014). *OIA annual report 2013.* Reading: Office of the Independent Adjudicator for Higher Education.

OIA. (2015). *Current case studies—Recent decisions of the OIA.* Retrieved February 18, 2015, from http://oiahe.org.uk/decisions-and-publications/recent-decisions-of-the-oia/current-case-studies.aspx.

Pring, R., & Pollard, A. (2011). *Education for all: Evidence from the past, principles for the future.* London: The ESRC Teaching & Learning Research Programme.

Randle, K., & Brady, N. (1997). Managerialism and professionalism in the 'cinderella service'. *Journal of Vocational Education & Training, 49*(1), 121–139.

Ratcliffe, R. (2012). *The Guardian—Rise in teachers off work with stress—and union warns of worse to come.* The Guardian. Retrieved March 14, 2015, from http://www.theguardian.com/education/2012/dec/26/teachers-stress-unions-strike.

Ritzner, G. (2012). *McDonaldization of society* (20th Anniversary ed.). London: Sage.

Robson, J. (2006). *Teacher professionalism in further and higher education.* Abingdon: Routledge.

Rowland, S. (2002). Overcoming fragmentation in professional life: The challenge for academic development. *Higher Education Quarterly, 56*(1), 52–64.

SAS. (2015). *Absence and maternity insurance.* Retrieved January 11, 2015, from http://www.schooladvice.co.uk/absence-and-maternity-insurance/staff-absence-insurance/.

Smith, A., Brice, C., Collins, A., Matthews, V., & McNamara, R. (2000). *The scale of occupational stress: A further analysis of the impact of demographic factors and type of job, HSE Report 311/2000.* Sudbury: The Health & Safety Executive.

Smith, K. (2012). Fools, facilitators and flexians: Academic identities in marketised environments. *Higher Education Quarterly, 66*(2), 155–173.

Soilemetzidis, I., Bennett, P., Buckley, A., Hillman, N., & Stoakes, G. (2014). *The HEPI–HEA student academic experience survey 2014*. York: Higher Education Academy.

Sparkes, A. (2007). Embodiment, academics, and the audit culture: A story seeking consideration. *Qualitative Research, 7*(4), 521–550.

UCU. (2014). *UCU Survey of Work-Related Stress 2014: Summary of findings by sector (HSE job-related hazards and psychological distress scores and a general picture of working hours only)*. London: The University and College Union.

University of California. (2015). *University of California: Expenditures for undergraduate and graduate instruction and research activities Oakland*. California: University of California.

Wall, T. (2013). *Professional identities and commodification in higher education*. Unpublished Doctoral Thesis, Manchester Metropolitan University, Manchester.

Whitchurch, C. (2008a). *Professional managers in UK higher education: Preparing for complex futures*. London: Leadership Foundation for Higher Education.

Whitchurch, C. (2008b). Shifting identities and blurring boundaries: The emergence of third space professionals in UK higher education. *Higher Education Quarterly, 62*(4), 377–396.

Whitchurch, C. (2009). The rise of the blended professional in higher education: A comparison between The United Kingdom, Australia and The United States. *Higher Education, 58*(3), 407–418.

Whitchurch, C. (2010). Some implications of 'public/private' space for professional identities in higher education. *Higher Education, 60*(6), 407–418.

Žižek, S. (1989). *The sublime object of ideology*. London: Verso.

Žižek, S. (1994). How did Marx invent the symptom? In S. Žižek (Ed.), *Mapping ideology* (pp. 296–331). London: Verso.

Žižek, S. (2000). *The fragile absolute: Or, why is the christian legacy worth fighting for?*. London: Verso.

Žižek, S. (2001). *The fright of real tears: Krzysztof Kieslowski between theory and post-theory*. Bloomington: Indiana University Press.

Žižek, S. (2002). *Enjoy your symptom! Jacques Lacan in Hollywood and out* (2nd ed.). London: Routledge.

Žižek, S. (2006). *The parallax view*. Cambridge, MA: MIT Press.

Žižek, S. (2008). *Violence*. London: Profile.

Žižek, S. (2009). *Denial: The Liberal Utopia*. http://www.lacan.com/essays/?page_id=397.

Žižek, S. (2014). *Trouble in paradise: From the end of history to the end of capitalism*. London: Allen Lane.

Chapter 5
We Know, *but Still*

Abstract As far as Žižek is concerned, our daily lives are intimately tainted and shaped by particular ideas and beliefs which implicate what we see, how we see, and therefore how we relate to each other in educational settings. Within contemporary educational settings, education is being cast in relation to economic utility. This activates particular expectations which generate educational customers and providers: now, in education, the 'Customer is King' at many different levels, from school to higher education. For Žižek, these ideas and beliefs have succeeded when we do not notice these particular shapes and forms, or when we do notice them and think they are 'natural', or that this is 'the way education is'. Žižek, however, warns us that the 'we do not know what we do' idiom is a faulty one, and does not explain why we can be acutely aware of the troubles in our so called educational paradise, but carry on regardless: we know the limitations of educational audits or student satisfaction surveys, but we spend extraordinary amount of time and effort preparing for them. Žižek's point here is that 'we do know, but still', through our behaviour, carry on. Being critical might appear to be a route to navigate this, but with a true Žižekian twist, can be a direct route for particular ideas and beliefs to take a tighter grip. In this way, such mechanics help to explain another dimension of why it is so challenging to achieve educational transformation on any level, from particular classroom teaching practices, through to the way education operates more broadly within society.

Keywords Disavowed belief · Normalisation · Naturalisation · Critical thinking · Cynical distance

Acting 'as if' 2 + 2 = 5

Was Orwell's '1984' a fiction about how the state was influencing people in ways so they believed 2 + 2 = 5? Or was it a commentary about ethnomathematical approaches to calculation, where it is quite possible for 2 + 2 = 5 when using

© The Author(s) 2015
T. Wall and D. Perrin, *Slavoj Žižek*,
SpringerBriefs on Key Thinkers in Education,
DOI 10.1007/978-3-319-21242-5_5

particular tools and mechanisms for addition? Perhaps it reflects a deeply Žižekian observation of a phenomenon which appears again and again in contemporary educational contexts where we may know $2 + 2 = 4$, but act 'as if' $2 + 2 = 5$, or more broadly, that our behaviour does not reflect what we openly say in front of colleagues—be it complaining about the quality in the latest coffee machine in the staff room (but then still drink it), or complaining about the latest amendment in a national curriculum (but then still teach it). As Butler explains in the context of money; "it does not matter that we know money is not an immediate expression of wealth… All that matters is that in our actual behaviour we continue to act *as though it is*" (Butler 2005, p. 5, emphasis added).

There are multiple examples that can be identified in contemporary education. In a major review of the National Student Survey in higher education, researchers concluded that:

> …stakeholders and students thought the NSS had conceptual *weaknesses* concerning what it measured, and methodological *weaknesses* related to what it covered. In particular, they were concerned that the NSS's scope was too *narrow* in terms of students' experiences and their engagement in learning and teaching which *undermined* the NSS's efficacy in informing student choice and enhancing students' academic experience. (HEFCE 2014, p. 3, emphasis added)

Why is it, then, that higher education professional across the country "*used* the NSS to help enhance the quality of their provision" (HEFCE 2014, p. 3), even though it was recognized as having multiple weaknesses? Even a recent research report by the Higher Education Academy points to the same phenomenon:

> Education is, of course, about a lot more than simply being 'provided' with teaching, resources and facilities. It is not a simple consumer relationship, but a partnership which requires effort and engagement from the student and it is the responsibility of their institution to encourage and facilitate this. *Nonetheless*, this survey provides us with an opportunity to investigate *their sense of value-for-money*… (Soilemetzidis et al. 2014, p. 33, emphasis added)

In other words, we know it is much more than the mis-recognition of customer-provider relationship, *but nonetheless*, we will do research into precisely this area. Is this not the same phenomenon as we witness in international research impact assessments in higher education establishments? Perhaps Sparkes (2007) pinpoints the spirit of the Žižekian point in his story of a researcher involved in such activity who feels compelled to give advice to his Vice-Chancellor:

> Vice-chancellor, can I just point out that this research assessment exercise stuff is a crock of shit. An absolute load of bollocks. I know it, you know it, we all know it. So why don't we just admit it and get on with something worthwhile? (Sparkes 2007, p. 526)

Primary school education does not escape this phenomenon. Do we not understand that Ofsted gradings are flawed and do not fully reflect pupil experience, or reflect the circumstances in which school teachers operate? Nonetheless, we still make changes to lesson plans, and even the structure of the entire school day, to ensure we get a good or better score. The National Union of Teachers tells us that 83 % of teachers say their most recent Ofsted inspection increases the pressure they experience and results in additional stress (NUT 2013). In other words, our behaviours indicate that we are acting 'as if' such inspections *do* reflect the experience of pupils and are crucially important.

To clarify the point here: this discussion is *not* about the reliability, validity or even utility of such scores, but it *is* about how we may publically acknowledge and critique an issue or problem, but at the same time, we carry on regardless—that is, we know something is unreliable, but we still use it 'as if' it is reliable. For Žižek, this is precisely how interpellation, as discussed in the previous chapter, works: the proverbial National Student Survey and Ofsted inspections are calling us from behind *'hey you!'* and we turn. This 'turn' happens when we re-direct investment, amend infrastructures, tweak learning and teaching strategies, and alter delivery patterns of courses in order to improve our scores. In other words, *in our behaviours, we are acting 'as if' they are reliable and important*—and, of course, we celebrate when we get a good score or improvement in it.

This magical trick can also extend its reach to educational innovations and reforms which appear to be radical breaks from dominant structures. One of the educational experiments over the last century has included educational forms under the broad 'free school' label, attempting to challenge dominant orthodoxies in sometimes very radical ways. Arguably the best known example has been A.S. Neill's Summerhill School founded in 1921 (Neill 1960). This school was, and still is, predicated on the idea that children flourish most when free from coercion: it is run on entirely democratic principles, with children deciding what they learn (in discussion with their tutors) and democratically establishing and enforcing any necessary rules and codes of behaviour, resolving disputes in school meetings.

For many decades Summerhill had an unhappy relationship with the UK educational authorities, with multiple attempts to close it in the late 1990s, mainly due to its lack of compulsory lessons. Eventually, the legal case against it brought by the schools' inspectorate Ofsted on behalf of the Blair government collapsed. Pupils from Summerhill who attended the court hearing later took over the courtroom to discuss the proposed settlement, to which they agreed (see the dramatized account in the 2008 BBC TV film *Summerhill*). Summerhill clearly breaks from dominant forms of education, but it still exists within a wider structure managed by government. Summerhill's last Ofsted inspection reveals specific ways in which the dominant expectations, which are not so radical, appear in the classroom:

> [Summerhill School] meets all the *regulatory requirements* for independent schools... The *national minimum standards* for boarding schools are met... The good *curriculum* is underpinned by effective written *policies* and *schemes* of work. *Planning* for lessons in all subjects is set out clearly with *units of work* that have clearly identified *objectives* and *resources*. (Ofsted 2011, emphasis added)

Within this very short extract, we see glimpses into the expectations of a standardised form of school education, shaped and governed by regulatory requirements, national standards, a curriculum, written policies, written schemes of work, lesson plans, units of work with specified objectives and resources. The

Žižekian twist here is that although we might aim for a radical departure, we might land at a place that is at least partially caught in the dominant perspective.

But is this not because of governmental imposition? You can see the same magical trick being performed in other contexts too, without governmental imposition. Other forms of 'free schools' flourished in the 1960s and 70s in cities across the UK, most notably the Free School in the downtrodden Scotland Road area of Liverpool, the London Free School in Notting Hill and the White Lion Street Free School in Islington. These owed much to Summerhill and the radical, hippy-influenced politics of the era, seeking to empower children who felt excluded from the orthodox state educational system. Few survived however, and often demonstrated their limitations as democratic and co-operative institutions operating within the wider prevailing norms of competitive, capitalist society. This experience at Scotland Road was not untypical, and demonstrates the trick at work:

> History meant visiting Welsh castles. And when workers at the local JCB factory in Kirkby went on strike, the pupils joined them for a sit-in. But the free ideology espoused by the adults was occasionally shot down by the children, such as the time when the girls *demanded a uniform.* Their "bourgeois" wish was granted, even when they asked for *checked lambswool miniskirts* from a particular boutique in Liverpool. The *request for matching coats* was politely declined. (de Castella 2014, emphasis added)

Here, the students, though wanting to be free from dominant forms of education, were caught by a desire for a uniform (to become standardised in terms of education) and checked lambswool miniskirts (to become standardised in terms of popular fashion). Contemporary free schools under David Cameron and Michael Gove have not been of the same ilk as these earlier versions, with criticisms that their greater freedom can promote sectional and orthodox interests, including religious ones (see some of the critiques here Garner 2015; Ofsted 2015).

But what about other radical departures, which might be labelled as alternative or even un-schooling (see the *Journal of Unschooling and Alternative Learning*, Nipissing University 2015)? For example, within Montessori educational approaches, particular learning outcomes and ways of knowing are not prescribed at the outset thereby enabling a much more personalised experience to the needs and interests of the individual (American Montessori Society 2015; Friersona 2014; Montessori 1965). Do these alternative approaches of education escape the bureaucratic frameworks described above?

Perhaps not: "Public Montessori schools are *mandated* to administer the same *standardized tests* as other public schools" and "some private Montessori schools also administer *standardized exams*, particularly if they will be required by schools into which their students may transition" (American Montessori Society 2015, emphasis added). In other words, though a radically different picture of education is painted, emphasising the personalised discovery and knowing, they are also caught in a wider system which understands education in a more bureaucratic sense where testing and examining particular constructs of learning are important and valued. We may want a new direction for education, but a wider system imposes itself, and we need it to if we are to exist within that system.

What about a return to the autodidactic (self-taught) tradition, where some Marxists claimed that 'knowledge is power' and those who wield it are powerful? This lead to conscious attempts at self-improvement outside of the formal educational system (Macintyre 1980). In essence, it was a product of opposition to the idea of capitalism's 'education factories', with schools and colleges growing up alongside the industrialisation and urbanisation associated with modern capitalism, being perceived as producing workers with the requisite skills and abilities to function as exploitable wage slaves in capitalist society. It was claimed that just as the early factories developed on Taylorist and Fordist principles of repeated processes, hierarchy and order, so did the schools—and eventually the universities too (initially for the elite but then generalised and now commodified in the modern era for larger sections of the working class). The autodidactic tradition stood outside these developments and challenged them, though was arguably a product of its time and heyday in the first half of the twentieth century.

To an extent, perhaps, this type of approach is currently being reinvigorated by the invention and explosion of Open Educational Resources (OER) such as Massive Open Online Courses (MOOCs)? OER as a phenomenon has opened the door to educational access that is not overtly defined by money-commodity relationships, and MOOCs give millions of people around the globe free access to Ivy League higher education courses in multiple subject areas, enabling them to construct their own learning from a vast menu of subjects, tailoring it to their needs and purposes. Is this not an alternative educational form? Again, Žižek might suggest not: many MOOCs are derived from on-campus higher education courses studied on campus, which are constructed within the realms of those highly regulated courses.

Here, we do not have to look far to see how these educational experiences are defined in terms of learning outcomes, learning hours, learning content, and even well-defined tactics for assessing learning—often in the form of 'multiple choice' questions which require the student to 'tick' boxes. Here, MOOCs could even be understood as an extension of the dominant form of higher education study packaged as discrete boxes. In true (dominant) form, at the end of their educational experience, the learner receives a certificate to prove they have completed the boxes as defined by the academic framework to which the university subscribes.

These contemporary cases exemplify the Žižekian critique of the Marxist idea that social change happens when we become aware of the problems in our working or life contexts, or how we are influenced by wider structures—that is, we are kept in place by the idea that 'we do not know what we do'. Žižek wants us to realise that we might know that findings from surveys are flawed, but we act as if they are not, and *still* use it to direct our action (2 + 2 = 5). He wants us to recognise that although we might assert a radical approach, our actions are still at least partially caught by a dominant regulative perspective (2 + 2 = 5).

But why would we possibly want to do such things, especially if it contributes to the troubles sketched out earlier, such as 'unacceptable levels of stress' and unpleasant complaints processes? Such logic is reminiscent of a twelfth century proverb *cutting my nose off to spite my face*, or perhaps a Chinese proverb *looking for a donkey while sitting on its back*. Is the answer not simple and obvious, that is, are we not compelled to act in such ways for economic reasons? Žižek goes further and points to how this works in the psyche, i.e. how capitalist ideology grips our mind in terms of our identity, propelling us in the ways constructed by the ideology. He argues that the answer is deeply embedded within our subjectivity, and why we do this returns us precisely to the earlier discussion of how we are compelled towards a simplified image of self in the Imaginary: every time I speak, a little "question mark" over what I have said appears because something escapes (Žižek 1989, p. 111), and I get pleasure from trying to capture a unified self, always failing, and therefore bracketing out any discrepancies. And this brings us to reiterate and reinforce the importance of the danger that Žižek warns us about: we should be wary about "the 'unknown knowns'—the disavowed beliefs, suppositions and obscene practices we pretend not to know about" (Žižek 2004).

On Being Critical (And Being Caught, Again)

It might seem that the solution lies in becoming aware of how the 'unknown knowns' shape and construct education, teachers and learners, perhaps through 'critical reflection'. For example, we might follow many other scholars who critique the gap that separates higher education from its customers (in the vein of Bolden et al. 2009, 2010; CBI 2008, 2009; Cooper et al. 2008; Garnett 2009; Garnett et al. 2008; Wedgewood 2008; White 2012). Our critical reflection might lead us to employ "good marketing and good project management techniques" (Cooper et al. 2008, p. 32), or employ brokerage or translation staff who can communicate in 'both' languages, and can understand and manage the different expectations of each world (Bolden et al. 2009; Dhillon et al. 2011; Workman 2010).

Or our critique might lead to more fundamental calls to action, which require a 'paradigm shift' towards a "widespread culture of engagement—of business focus, of 'close connect' with professional employment and practice", and specifically a culture "permeating all aspects of provision from the business model of a [higher education institution], through... new pedagogies for workforce education, to individual employment contracts for HE staff" (Wedgewood 2008, p. 20). Yet such actions, where implemented, might not *practically* change anything of significance, because they are not changing the wider forces outside any particular educational organisation or body (Gibbs and Garnett 2007). For Žižek, these acts are not addressing the Symbolic order which is setting up the 'student as customer' notion and which activates particular expectations which infiltrate relationships in the educational context.

Even if we do begin to question the 'student as customer' notion, which publications such as this book might aspire to do, we are doing so only within the structures and terms of the language that was used to set up such notions in the first place. In this way, we are being tricked into thinking we are surpassing the Symbolic realm, but we are in effect (through our behaviour) fully in accordance with the terms of a particular perspective that is reinforced by the dominant discourse. And in so doing, we are still activating all of the associated unconscious motivations described earlier. Žižek refers to this as 'cynical distance', and rather than creating distance, dialectically, it is a requirements for such notions to grip us. He says that thinking we are "stepping out of (what we experience as) ideology is the very form of our enslavement to it" (Žižek 1994, p. 6).

Importantly, "those who do not let themselves be caught in the symbolic/fiction and continue to believe their eyes are the ones who err most" (Žižek 2005), or in other words, those who *think* they are *not* caught by ideological framing, and then continue to believe what they see, *are* already caught. In such circumstances, as the Chinese proverbs tell us, our attempts at critical reflection become like gazing at a plum to quench our thirst or hitting a dog with a meat bun to protect ourselves. Such attempts reflect what happens to us when we are dealing with fetishes, that is, the fantasy versions of objects that have become commodified:

> while the fundamentalist ignores (or at least mistrusts) argumentation, blindly clinging to his fetish, the cynic pretends to accept argumentation, but ignores its symbolic efficiency. In others words, while the fundamentalist (not so much believes as) directly 'knows' the truth embodies in his fetish, the cynic practises the logic of disavowal ('I know very well, but...'). (Žižek 2009, pp. 68–69)

But how is it the Symbolic works so efficiently in this way? We have already heard Žižek's explanations about how we are motivated to think in particular ways, but when we are dealing with educational fetishes, are we really that 'blind' not to see the difference between the proverbial MBA and 12,000 Big Mac meals? Surely we can see that we sitting on the proverbial donkey when we are trying to find it? Importantly, Žižek argues that the Real is parallactic in the sense we only ever get glimpses of the same 'thing' from different angles which generates a "multiplicity of appearances" (Žižek 2006, p. 26). In other words, because of the unknowability of the Real, we are able to see and make sense of objects from different angles or from different perspectives. Collini exemplifies this in the context of education, about himself, also known as 'the parallactic Collini':

> I work in the knowledge and human-resources industry. My company specializes in two kinds of product: we manufacture high-quality, multi-skilled units of human capacity; and we produce commercially relevant, cutting-edge new knowledge in user-friendly packaged of printed material... Let me put that another way. I'm a university teacher. I teach students and I write books... I teach at a British university. (Collini 2012, p. 132)

In terms of education, we have already discussed this in terms of saleable product forms, and in terms of bureaucratic forms (credits, levels, units, modules, programmes). A cynical engagement here might ask; which one is the real form of education? The problem is that there is no neutral answer, and the point is that things are "continuous with each other: the one, as it is, is the "truth" of the other, and vice versa" (Žižek 2007). In other words, the point is that we can never seize the Real, but we can only access glimpses or appearances of partial bits of it—"our vision of reality is anamorphically distorted... [and that this] accounts for the very *multiplicity* of appearances of the same underlying Real" (Žižek 2006, p. 26). What is more, the appearances that do see are always already shaped by the same desires that are mobilising our motivations:

> [an] object assumes clear and distinctive features only if we look at it "at an angle", i.e. with an "interested" view, supported, permeated, and "distorted" by *desire*... an object that be perceived only by a gaze "distorted" by desire, an object that *does not exist* for an "objective" gaze... outside this distortion, "in itself", *it does not exist*, since it is *nothing but* the embodiment, the materialization of this very distortion... "objectively" nothing, though, viewed from a certain perspective, it assumes the shape of "something". (Žižek 1991, p. 12)

In other words, for something to exist or to be subjectively experienced, it must be framed (in the first place) by a desire: a particular (so called, distorted) perspective is required by a spectator to see some-thing. As such, parallax gaps can occur: when two perspectives exist where there is an "antinomy which can never be dialectically "mediated/sublated" into a higher synthesis, since there is no common language, no shared ground" (Žižek 2006, p. 4). For Žižek, these are all around us, but we may not recognise them as such. One unsettling example can be spotted in the narratives used to describe Josef Fritzl—from one angle (in media accounts), he was represented as a *monster* who did terrible and unthinkable things to his family, and from another angle (in his own accounts), he was the opposite, a *loving* father who was protecting his family from the dangers of the modern world (Žižek 2008, p. ix). These are different ways of understanding the same 'thing' of 'Josef Fritzl', but which cannot be reconciled.

This is the same sort of tension that arises when we understand education as a commercial product form (a Best Buy) compared with its bureaucratic terms (credits and levels)—when such forms appear as alternatives, they appear as incompatible or incommensurate. The discussion above suggests, however, that they are 'continuous', but in what way? Perhaps this text from a real advertisement for a higher education establishment in New York gives us a dialectical clue:

Question: Why study in Puerto Rico?

Answer: lower cost per credit!

Is this advert not a signal that shows that a consumerist packaging of higher education as a product is *absolutely not at odds* with a bureaucratic packaging into academic credits? Here, it is not that it is oppositional at all, but that the former is dependent on and realised *precisely because of the latter*? In other words, we are able to package a product precisely because we have credits. Indeed, through a long drawn-out and uneven process (Betts and Smith 1998), academic 'credit' has emerged as the key measure and store of value when education is packaged into units of study. In many respects, credit in the academic sphere reflects the volume of learning required to demonstrate achievement from students in a similar way to how Marx explained the exchange value of commodities in capitalism on the basis of the average amount of labour time needed from workers to produce them from start to finish. And these education credits—the product of the labours of learning—are similarly intended to be as interchangeable as possible, being capable of importation from one course to another under certain conditions through the recognition of prior learning (Perrin and Helyer 2015). In effect, the units become a universal educational currency, or 'money', which is recognised across a system.

In the UK for example, the credit system involves 10 hours of learning being the 'universal equivalent' of one credit point, with Europe more generally being based on the equivalence of 20 hours of learning for one credit. Now part of a global educational trend, each qualification of worth is defined in terms of an academic level and credit value. So value, volume and equivalence are crucial (Perrin and Helyer 2015), just as they were for Marx when explaining the exchange value of physical commodities in capitalism.

Much of the language of HE now reflects this widespread commodification and monetisation. For instance, when students are asked to show that their prior learning is still up-to-date and reflects contemporary thinking it is called demonstrating 'currency'. Similarly, achieved credit is in 'the bank' and they may choose to achieve other credits through taking units of study (modules) from 'the bank of modules' on offer. This Symbolic order of higher education impacts on the consciousness of academics and students alike, and reflects dialectical contradictions within the way education and wider society relate to one another.

This dialectical twist is just as evident in radical higher education programmes which are designed on the fundamental principle of negotiation between the learner and the higher education establishment, rather than pre-set criteria and methods of learning and assessment (see for example Aditomo et al. 2011; Boud and Solomon 2001; Wall 2010; Workman et al. 2009; Lester and Costley 2010; Mabweazara and Taylor 2012). One example is 'negotiated work based learning' where learners are able to negotiate programmes of study that relate to them and their workplace, often being based on a combination of prior and current experiential learning through work. Such programmes typically aim to:

- enable widening participation opportunities for adult learners who normally would not or could not attend university,
- allow students to take responsibility for their own learning within certain parameters, such as enabling negotiation of learning pathways, module content (for example, through work based projects), and even award titles that reflect the area of working practice,
- emphasise opportunities for the accreditation of prior learning, both experiential and certificated,
- enhance professional development and workplace capability, and
- provide for the possible accreditation of in-house training programmes delivered by other organisations, such as companies (Perrin et al. 2009).

On the one hand, such programmes are a manifestation of ultimate flexibility, attempting to break free from the dominant approach to higher education study that has been prescriptive and academy-led. In doing so, they attempt to empower learners to negotiate the educational focus, content and structure of their own learning (often written by *them* rather than the academics). Such a way of working even involves a very different power relationship between tutor and student than in other programmes, with students taking much more 'ownership' and 'control' of their learning (Talbot 2010; Wall 2013). Yet on the other hand, to exercise their choice, learners have to engage considerably with—and understand—these constructs far more than other students need to.

Although engaging with the bureaucracy of such academic frameworks can be alien, frustrating and confusing for learners—especially the administrative processes associated with it—this level of choice is facilitated *precisely because of* the existence of the underlying academic framework that governs it: precisely defined academic levels and credits provide a currency system on which to deliver the flexibility. In this way, learners (and their tutors) become 'credit mechanics', fully immersed in a particular way of packaging education. So rather than being on two different hands, it might be better expressed as two sides of the same (academic) coin.

Žižek might also want us to notice another dialectical twist about negotiated higher education study which emphasises an earlier point. The basis for this type of education emerged during the free-spirited 1960s (such as with the Open University in the UK), representing an attempt to democratise education and empower students, often using ideas which scholars describe as potentially subversive at work (Brookfield 1991). Yet part of the function of this type of education is set within the context of enhancing professional practices, focusing on improving the production of ever more efficient wage slaves. Indeed, negotiated work based learning enables the co-creation of learning between workers, but also with the companies employing them: all mediated, packaged, and assessed through the universal HE credit system, most notably and obviously where it involves the negotiation of bespoke corporate programmes. So in this way, although it was an attempt to break with traditional approaches of higher education, it can immerse students and staff even more deeply into capitalist structures than perhaps other forms of higher education study.

In this vein, such forms of higher education study can be seen as an innovative and far-reaching mechanism that can enable a particular form of education to impact on sectors and people that would not otherwise be enveloped by such processes—or alternatively expressed, extend into 'hard to reach' parts of society. In this respect, it is the ultimate expression of higher education packaged as credits despite its radical and empowering aspirations. So in this Žižekian sense one of the most radical, challenging and potentially subversive educational approaches that has been developed in the modern era also contains within it something of its opposite—the standard, the conforming, the ordered and the privatised. So what is to be done to navigate such insidious mechanisms, or realise that we are sitting on the donkey we are looking for? This is the focus of our final chapter, next.

References

Aditomo, A., Goodyear, P., Bliuc, A. M., & Ellis, R. A. (2011). Inquiry-based learning in higher education: Principal forms, educational objectives, and disciplinary variations. *Studies in Higher Education, 38*(9), 1239–1258.

American Montessori Society. (2015). *Frequently asked questions*. Retrieved March 14, 2015, from http://amshq.org/Montessori-Education/FAQs.

Betts, M., & Smith, R. (1998). *Developing the credit-based modular curriculum in higher education: Challenge, choice and change*. London: Routledge.

Bolden, R., Connor, H., Duquemin, A., Hirsh, W., & Petrov, G. (2009). *Employer engagement with higher education: Defining, sustaining, and supporting higher skills provision*. London: Department for Innovation, Universities and Skills.

Bolden, R., Hirsh, W., Connor, H., Petrov, G., & Duquemin, A. (2010). *Strategies for effective HE-employer engagement*. London: Department for Innovation, Universities and Skills.

Boud, D., & Solomon, N. (2001). Repositioning universities and work. In D. Boud & N. Solomon (Eds.), *Work based learning: A new higher education?*. Buckingham: Open University Press.

Brookfield, S. D. (1991). *Developing critical thinkers: Challenging adults to explore alternative ways of thinking and acting*. San Francisco: Jossey-Bass.

Butler, R. (2005). *Slavoj Žižek: Live Theory*. London: Continuum.

CBI. (2008). *Stepping higher: Workforce development through employer-higher education partnership*. London: Confederation of British Industry.

CBI. (2009). *Stronger together: Businesses and universities in turbulent times*. London: Department for Business, Innovation and Skills.

Collini, S. (2012). *What are universities for*? London: Penguin.

Cooper, C., Mackinnon, I., & Garside, P. (2008). *Employer engagement research report 29*. Wath-upon-Dearne: Sector Skills Development Agency.

de Castella, T. (2014). *BBC News—The anarchic experimental schools of the 1970s*. Retrieved March 14, 2015, from http://www.bbc.co.uk/news/magazine-29518319.

Dhillon, B., Edmonds, T., Felce, A., Minton, A., & Wall, T. (2011). *Making employer and university partnerships work: Accredited employer-led learning*. Faringdon: Libri Publishing.

Friersona, P. R. (2014). Maria Montessori's epistemology. *British Journal for the History of Philosophy, 22*(4), 767–791.

Garner, R. (2015). *The independent—Free school praised by Michael Gove ordered to close due to bullying and religious bigotry*. Retrieved March14, 2015, from, http://www.independent.co.uk/news/education/free-school-praised-by-michael-gove-ordered-to-close-due-to-bullying-and-religious-bigotry-9988859.html.

Garnett, J. (2009). Contributing to the intellectual capital of organisations. In J. Garnett, C. Costley, & B. Workman (Eds.), *Work based learning: Journeys to the core of higher education*. London: Middlesex University Press.

Garnett, J., Workman, B., Beadsmoore, A., & Bezencenet, S. (2008). Developing the structural capital of higher education institutions to support work based learning. In F. Tallantyre (Ed.), *Work-based learning: Workforce development: Connections, frameworks and processes* (pp. 18–30). York: The Higher Education Academy.

Gibbs, P., & Garnett, J. (2007). Work-based learning as a field of study. *Research in Post-Compulsory Education, 12*(3), 409–421.

HEFCE. (2014). *Review of the national student survey report to the UK higher education funding bodies by NatCen Social Research, the Institute of Education, University of London and the Institute for Employment Studies: Summary Report*. London: Higher Education Funding Council for England.

Lester, S., & Costley, C. (2010). Work-based learning at higher education level: Value, practice and critique. *Studies in Higher Education, 35*(5), 561–575. doi:10.1080/03075070903216635.

Mabweazara, H. M., & Taylor, A. (2012). Exploring effective pedagogies for delivering journalism work-based learning in UK higher education. *Journal of Media Practice, 13*(2), 125–142.

Macintyre, S. (1980). *A proletarian science*. Cambridge: Cambridge University Press.

Montessori, M. (1965). *The Montessori method: Scientific pedagogy as applied to child education in "The children's houses", with additions and revisions by the author*. (Anne E. George (Italian), Trans.). Cambridge, MA: Robert Bentley.

Neill, A. S. (1960). *Summerhill: A radical approach to child rearing*. New York: Hart Publishing Co., Inc.

Nipissing University. (2015). *Journal of Unschooling and Alternative Learning.* Retrieved March 14, 2015, from http://jual.nipissingu.ca/.

NUT. (2013). *Teacher Stress: NUT guidance to divisions and associations.* London: The National Union of Teachers.

Ofsted. (2011). *Summerhill school—Independent school standard inspection report.* Manchester: The Office for Standards in Education, Children's Services and Skills.

Ofsted. (2015). *The Durham free school—School inspection report.* Manchester: The Office for Standards in Education, Children's Services and Skills.

Perrin, D., & Helyer, R. (2015). Make your learning count: Recognition of prior learning. In R. Helyer (Ed.), *The work based learning student handbook.* Basingstoke: Palgrave Macmillan.

Perrin, D., Weston, P., Thompson, P., & Brodie, P. (2009). *Facilitating em-ployer engagement through negotiated work based learning.* Bristol: Higher Education Funding Council for England.

Soilemetzidis, I., Bennett, P., Buckley, A., Hillman, N., & Stoakes, G. (2014). *The HEPI–HEA student academic experience survey 2014.* York: Higher Education Academy.

Sparkes, A. (2007). Embodiment, academics, and the audit culture: A story seeking consideration. *Qualitative Research, 7*(4), 521–550.

Talbot, J. (2010). Changing power relations in work based learning: Collaborative and contested relations between tutors, learners and employers. In S. Jackson (Ed.), *Innovations in lifelong learning* (pp. 187–208). London: Routledge.

Wall, T. (2010). University models of work-based learning validation. In J. Mumford & S. Roodhouse (Eds.), *Understanding work-based learning* (pp. 41–54). London: Gower.

Wall, T. (2013). Diversity through negotiation. In K. Bridger, I. Reid, & J. Shaw (Eds.), *Inclusive higher education: An International perspective on access and the challenge of student diversity.* Faringdon: Libri Publishing.

Wedgewood, M. (2008). *Higher education for the workforce—Barriers and facilitators to employer engagement.* London: Department for Innovation, Universities and Skills.

White, T. (2012). Employer responsive provision: Workforce development through work-based learning. *Higher Education, Skills and Work-based Learning, 2*(1), 6–21.

Workman, B. (2010). University challenge: Learning to work with employer engagement. *Educational Developments, 11*(2), 9–12.

Workman, B., Costley, C., & Garnett, J. (2009). *Work-based learning journeys to the core of higher educations.* London: Middlesex University Press.

Žižek, S. (1989). *The sublime object of ideology.* London: Verso.

Žižek, S. (1991). *Looking awry: An introduction to Jacques Lacan through popular culture.* London: The MIT Press.

Žižek, S. (1994). The spectre of ideology. In S. Žižek (Ed.), *Mapping ideology* (pp. 1–33). London: Verso.

Žižek, S. (2004). www.lacan.com—*What Rumsfeld doesn't know that he knows about Abu Ghraib.* Retrieved March 14, 2015, from http://www.lacan.com/zizekrumsfeld.htm.

Žižek, S. (2005). *With or without passion, whats wrong with fundamentalism?—Part I.* Retrieved August 26, 2013, from http://www.lacan.com/zizpassion.htm.

Žižek, S. (2006). *The parallax view.* Cambridge, MA: MIT Press.

Žižek, S. (2007). Digression 2—How to make a mobius strip. http://the-zizek-site.blogspot.co.uk/2007/01/digression-2-how-to-make-mobius-strip.html.

Žižek, S. (2008). *The plague of fantasies* (2nd ed.). London: Verso.

Žižek, S. (2009). *First tragedy, then as farce.* London: Verso.

Chapter 6
Now What *Might* We Do?

Abstract Žižek warns us that that we become enslaved to particular ideas and beliefs which implicate our inner-most unconscious desires and drives. Dialectically, being 'critical' about these ideas can work as an insidious way for such ideas to tighten their grip. So what can teachers and students do to bring about something else? Can we escape enslavery? For Žižek, we cannot escape the very Symbolic which guides us in knowing how to act in practice, and which manifests throughout vast educational and broader regulatory systems. So whatcan we do? This, Žižek points out, is our task rather than his, and refuses to provide specific actions for us—and is this not fully aligned to a slippery 'hag fish' pedagogy where we have to find the answers? Crucially, Žižek raises the urgency of a need to act, and gives us glimpses into directions that we might consider. Educational researchers have taken Žižek's inspiration and call to action, and have documented how they have constructed alternative actions in practice. Their interpretations have involved attempting to draw from different zones of the Symbolic realm, and patiently considering how such activity appears to be implicating themselves and others in their educational practices. Yet these are never definitive, victory narratives, as Žižek reminds us of Lacan's famous statement "les non-dupes errent": only those who think they have not been duped have already been duped. Such attempts do act, however, as beacons towards producing different understandings of education, and therefore hold the potential for change.

Keywords Act · Event · Master · Division · Les non-dupes errent

We Need to Act

This book has attempted to capture glimpses into contemporary education, in terms of how it is understood and how people such as educators, learners and the managers, think they should engage with it. These glimpses will always fail to capture

© The Author(s) 2015
T. Wall and D. Perrin, *Slavoj Žižek*,
SpringerBriefs on Key Thinkers in Education,
DOI 10.1007/978-3-319-21242-5_6

something because of the partiality of language and the unknowability of the Real, but they do provide points of reference for us all to consider, regardless of educational sector. Yet they are also glimpses into a situation that Žižek expresses his deep concern about, and this is perhaps articulated most succinctly in one of the very rare statements he makes directly about education:

> What has happened in the latest stage of post-68 capitalism is that the economy itself - the logic of market and competition - has progressively imposed itself as the hegemonic ideology. In education, we are witnessing the gradual dismantling… the school system is less and less the compulsory network, elevated above the market and organized directly by the state, bearer of enlightened values—liberty, equality, fraternity. On behalf of the sacred formula of 'lower costs, higher efficiency', it is progressively penetrated by different forms of ppp, or public–private partnership. (Žižek 2010, p. 91)

His argument is that previously the school system was a key means by which power divisions between the 'haves' and 'have nots', and various forms of inequality in society, were structured and maintained—similar to the explanations of class reproduction (see Bourdieu 1988). Now, however, Žižek is suggesting that the forces of educational privatisation and exposure to market forces are entrenching and infecting whole educational systems in other deeply insidious ways. This book, for example, illustrates many examples, such as the marketisation of education from academy school provision through to higher education, or a trend of "directly subordinat[ing] education to the demands of the market" (Žižek 2014b, p. 23). Žižek is particularly critical of these trends in higher education, especially the attempts through the Bologna Process to harmonize higher education systems in Europe. He sees this move as a 'concerted attack on the public use of reason' (Žižek 2010, p. 90; 2014b, p. 57), by which he means a kind of redirecting of education and knowledge towards narrow economic utility rather than for a wider social good. He says:

> Underlying these reforms is the urge to subordinate higher education to the task of solving society's concrete problems through the production of expert opinions. What disappears here is the true task of thinking: not only to offer solutions to problems posed by 'society'… but to reflect on the very form of these problems; to discern a problem in the very way we perceive a problem. The reduction of higher education to the task of producing socially useful expert knowledge is the paradigmatic form of Kant's 'private use of reason'—that is, constrained by contingent, dogmatic presuppositions… the process of enclosing the commons of intellectual products, of privatizing general intellect. (Žižek 2010, pp. 90–91)

Žižek's analysis here can be connected with Furedi's staunch defence of libertarian attitudes in an age where he feels civil liberties are under sustained threat from both anti-scientific superstition and an increasingly authoritarian state (Furedi 2006, 2010). For Furedi, modern higher education is obsessed with 'inclusivity' and 'widening access' at the expense of intellectual rigour, with a parallel undermining of the academic as an arbiter of critical analysis, taste and worthy ideas. Alternatively expressed, these equate to a critique of the 'dumbing down of educational standards' and a 'culture of flattery' (Furedi 2006, 2010). And though not explicit (see Žižek in Mariborchan.si 2014), it would seem that Žižek and Furedi are united forces against the attitude that the pursuit of knowledge for its own sake is "a bit dodgy" (to cite the then Secretary of State for Education in the UK Charles Clarke, Vasagar and Smithers 2003). Instead, according to both Žižek and Furedi, current conditions mean that education must now justify itself in terms of the economic benefits it provides to its stakeholders.

Does this mean instead that Žižek is suggesting a return to educational movements and organisations we have already seen in Europe, where voluntary associations and mass political movements have a role (see Steele 2015)? Going beyond the concepts of 'free schools' or similar, is he calling for arrangements akin to how the German Social Democratic Party in the late nineteenth and early twentieth centuries, the Workers' Educational Association (WEA) from the early 1900s, and later the National Council of Labour Colleges, organised and mobilised education (see Rose 2002)?

Or is Žižek suggesting other models, which have a more expressly political remit, not set up as competitors to the type of education typically promoted within higher education, but almost in antagonism to it? In the UK, for example, such organisations have included the Independent Labour Party (1893), the Socialist Labour Party (1903) and the still active Socialist Party of Great Britain (1904). Particularly in the last two organisations, education classes and the curricula underpinning them were explicitly set up as an anti-capitalist alternative to the fare offered by the universities and trade union-sponsored movements like the WEA and they were sometimes referred to by Marxists as the 'universities of the working class' for this reason. To use William Morris's phrase, their role was conceived as being about 'making socialists' through political education, in doing so hastening a revolutionary transformation of society (see Barltrop 1975; Perrin 2000).

Perhaps Žižek's own position is more precisely about calling us to take action without this degree of precision, and without the certainly or security of what might happen as a result:

> Today we do not know what we have to do, but we have to act now, because the consequence of non-action could be disastrous… We will have to risk taking steps into the abyss, in totally inappropriate situations. (Žižek 2010, p. 95)

So where does this leave us? How does this help us on our quest to change the situation should we feel a burning or tingling desire to? Perhaps underpinning this question is precisely what Žižek is trying to provoke and disrupt in his analysis: contemporary capitalism has extended its reach into education where we have to package up digestible answers for public consumption, or perhaps more specifically, for customers to consume (including the customer who buys this book). Is this not precisely why we have the '…for dummies' brand with its Symbolically revealing strap lines of "making everything easier" and "how-to's and advice from experts" (For Dummies 2015)? But let us not be tricked here: there is more than a very real possibility that a 'Žižek for dummies' is added to the 2,600 strong collection listed on their website very soon—has Springer not already beaten Wiley to it to publish the Žižekian Look at Education as a Springer Brief? This returns us to the very real status of the joke that introduced this book where people are driven to attend and consume a seminar to learn 'how to create a social revolution in 30 minutes'.

That said, we might be able to glean possible ideas of what we *can* do in some of the statements which have angered his critics. What can we learn, for example, in Žižek's public statement "I hate students, they are (as all people) mostly stupid and boring" (Greenstreet 2008). Is this to be read as a genuine, accurate statement of what he really thinks about his students? This certainly riles some of us enough to write articles about our anger and frustration especially when Žižek is heralded as so significant (Schuman 2014; Wolters 2014). Or might it be read as a statement to disrupt the very customer-provider relationship that is so prevalent in educational contexts, as discussed throughout this book? In other words, is Žižek's statement a carefully crafted 'situation' to try to stimulate a change in how something is understood? In this sense, it has a distinctly Situationist flavour to it.

We are not endorsing declaring our fictional 'hatred' of students or managers, or our fictional belief that students and managers are 'stupid and boring', but perhaps there is some value in entertaining the thought that there may be the germ of an idea there. Perhaps it is a seed that can even help us grow the possibility of finding new ways to relate to each other in educational settings. In this way, our attitude of engagement with Žižek is not one where we are expecting or demanding 'practical solutions', which is a popular criticism of his approach (Taylor 2010). Returning to the Žižekian critique above, this would be living out the construction of education as 'producing socially useful expert knowledge', or 'how to create a social revolution in 30 min'. As Žižek says:

> I always emphasise: don't expect this from me. I don't think that the task of a guy like me is to propose complete solutions. When people ask me what to do with the economy, what the hell do I know? I think the task of people like me is not to provide answers but to ask the right questions…(Žižek in Aitkenhead 2012)

This, indeed, is the kernel of Žižek's approach.

Glimpses into Navigating Differently

On that purposely unhelpful note, what are the supposedly valuable seeds that might give us insights into what we *can* do to change things in practice? Let's return to the statement "I hate students… they are mostly stupid and boring". This statement can perhaps be read as a possible manoeuvre which raises a question about the extent to which we are subscribing to the Symbolic which constructs students as 'Customer is King'. Here, this alerts us to the possibility of a radical act being to not engaging in a particular zone of the Symbolic. As Žižek says:

> (non)activity undermines the master's charisma, suspends the effect of 'quilting', and thus renders visible the distance that separates the master from the place he occupies. (Žižek 2002, p. 103)

In other words, by not engaging in the precise Symbolic constructions, it can undermine the expectations that are set up when we understand education as a commercial product for sale. In this sense, we might navigate the Symbolic in ways without "direct confrontation" with the power structures in place, but undermine those structures "in power with patient ideologico-critical work, so that although they are still in power, one all of a sudden notices that the powers-that-be are afflicted with unnaturally high voices" (Žižek 2009, p. 7).

To clarify, this 'patient' work is not about evacuating language and its representation by escaping the Symbolic: an earlier chapter explained that we need these structures to engage in reality and without them would be psychic breakdown. This is why Lacan says that drawing from the Symbolic is a matter of "a choice between 'bad' and 'worse'" (Žižek 2002, p. 75). Rather, this 'patient' work might mean being aware of the points of "original entry into the symbolic and reliv[ing] it as though it has not already taken place" (Butler 2005, p. 19). The point here is that although we cannot live 'outside' of Symbolic constructions (Žižek 1994, p. 19), we can choose our designations which activate a different "designate place in the intersubjective network" (Žižek 2002, p. 76).

In other words, we can consider alternative ways of drawing from the Symbolic which in turn potentially implicates us in different directions and therefore mobilises different expectations (in the ways discussed in the previous chapters). Because what escapes capture from the Symbolic exists in the Real, drawing on the Symbolic in different ways (or different zones of it) generates the possibility of activating other actions which might influence what happens in the Real. Žižek says:

> The Lacanian impossible-real is not an a priori limitation, which needs to be realistically taken into account, but the domain of action. An act is more than an intervention into the domain of the possible—an act changes the very coordinates of what is possible. (Žižek 2010, p. 94)

To be able to draw differently from the Symbolic, Žižek argues that it is crucial to recognise two particular but interconnected fictions. The first is that the unitary self is a fiction, driven by the avoidance of lack and fragmentation, and is not a neutral or naturally occurring object as such—the real totality of 'me' is that I am not a teacher, corporate consultant, student, and so on (in the Real, 'me' is not a unified thing). This is the realm of the Imaginary, shaped by the Symbolic and kept in place by desire hiding in the Real. The second fiction is what Žižek calls the Big Other, or the coherent embodiment of rules and laws, emerging from an unconscious desire to create some-thing from an object which is no-thing (i.e. constructed by the Symbolic, again to avoid lack). It is that which has already been evoked when *I feel I need to* make my classes more entertaining. As Žižek argues:

> the field of social practices and socially held beliefs is not just simply at a different level from the individual experience, but something to which *the individual him/herself has to relate*, which *the individual himself* has to experience as an order which is minimally 'reified', externalized... [it] *exists only insofar as individuals treat it as such, relate to it as such.* (Žižek 2006, p. 6, original emphasis)

In other words, the expectations activated when we conceive of education as a product to be sold only have power for as long as we unconsciously believe in them. For example, he says, "The status of the same person... can appear in an entirely different light the moment the modality of his/her relationship to the big Other changes" (Žižek 1999, p. 330). When we believe that the customer-provider relationship is not the natural or only way of existing, and we believe something else (whatever that might be), other expectations are potentially activated and we are driven in new directions.

This connects with the wider call by Bolden et al. (2009, p. 36) for "academic staff [to be] willing to consider different understandings of their role", even not if necessarily in the ways they suggest. The task is to ascertain the extent to which our alternative ways of drawing from the Symbolic trick us into *deepening* desires and drives to be customer focused and customer driven. For example, Barnett (2000, 2003, 2011) and Wedgewood (2008) attempt to re-conceptualise academic professionalism around the ideas of 'engagement' and the 'engagement for the freedom of others'. The problem is, however, are these, through our *practical action*, any different to framing the learner as a customer and the educator as the service provider? For Žižek, recall, we need to put on our critico-ideological glasses and look closely at our practical actions, even if we get a strong headache (Žižek 2013a).

Educational researchers have interpreted and operationalised these ideas in their own educational contexts and practice (for example, see: Brown 2008; Smith et al. 2013; Pais 2011; Brown et al. 2006; Bradford and Brown 2005; Brown and England 2005; Brown and Jones 2001; Brown and McNamara 2011; Brown and Walshaw 2012; Wall 2013; Cooley 2009; Meakin and Wall 2013; Yunkaporta and Kirby 2011). One flavour of practitioner research that has emerged involves practitioners closely examining their practice and monitoring effects through the narratives they tell about their practice. Here, research is fuelled by a continuous story telling process, a "reflective/constructive narrative layer that feeds whilst growing alongside the life it seeks to portray" (Brown and Jones 2001, p. 443).

To clarify, this is not necessarily with the aspiration to find and then correct 'distorted' perceptions (Habermas 1976), as Žižek might align with other scholars to question the possibility of this (Ricoeur 1984; Foucault 1980). Rather, it propels a Žižekian-infused curiosity about what appears be happening and how to construct the next professional manoeuvre. For example, it revolves around professionally constructed narratives:

> I may wish to share my thoughts spoken or written. But as I say something, I may be more or less disappointed with how my thoughts sounds once converted into words. And through my attempts to reconcile what I thought with what I said, my understanding of the world might then be modified. So when I feel ready to speak again, there may be some shift in the way in which I express myself, as, in a sense, a different person is speaking. And so on... where understandings and explanations continue to disturb each other perhaps for as long as I live. (Brown 2008, p. 405)

By connecting with different notions from the Symbolic realm, we are effectively able to create multiple and specific demands in different directions, each activating different expectations of how we think we should act. But what might 'patient ideologico-critical work' look like in practice to loosen the grip of the Symbolic in our daily lives? In one study, Wall (2013) found that some students studying two subjects at a university were sharing narratives of feeling like 'second class citizens'. In trying to address this, he found that such programmes were being conceptualised as 'two halves of two subjects', and by implication, not studying any 'full' subject. In tackling this representation, the researcher reformulated the 'two-halves-of-two-subjects' framework as a framework which specified a singular 'pathway'—thereby drawing from another zone of the Symbolic. Over time, there appeared to be indications that the way teachers conceptualised and related to the 'two subject' pathways had shifted towards 'coherent pathways' rather than 'jointness-as-halfness'. In a similar study, academics experimented with intentionally re-conceptualising their role in working with corporate organisations, away from a 'client advisor' towards 'learning partner' (Meakin and Wall 2013). Again, drawing differently from the Symbolic appeared to shape their daily interactions towards greater dialogue (rather than providing a service as such), and re-locate discussions around learning, play, and experimentation. Yet they were also aware of the boundaries to their experimentations whilst under the conditions of employment (see also England 2003, who found something similar in the context of primary education).

It might be forgivable to think that there is flexibility to experiment with different understanding of identities within the field of human relationships, given the nature of 'floating signifiers' (Žižek 1989, p. 95). But what about areas of education which might appear to be much more 'fixed', such as mathematical constructs? To think this would be understandable given that mathematics knowledge is considered to be "constituted by pre-existing patterns that are stable and are able to be discovered... [thus] it is possible to know what is and what is not true since knowledge is objective and universal" (Brown and Walshaw 2012, p. 2). Or, to return to the calculation we have already introduced in the previous chapter, is it not true that that $2 + 2 = 4$?

A central tenet of Žižek's argument is aligned with Orwell's assertion of how wider societal structures can be in place which mean $2 + 2 = 5$. Both calculations ($2 + 2 = 4$ and $2 + 2 = 5$) can be understood to be accurate, shaped by the context in which they are made, for example, the specific tools used within such calculations (see Kaino 2013). To illustrate: it may well be acceptable to calculate $2 + 2$ using two cords: I place two knots on one cord, and then two knots on another cord, and then add the two cords together with another knot, ergo, I have 5 knots altogether. That is, $2 + 2 = 5$. This is why some scholars interpret "ethnomathematics as a model for translating and interpreting mathematical structures inherent in existing indigenous technologies" (Chahine and Kinuthia 2013, p. 1). In other words, even constructs of mathematical knowledge are subject to the slippery nature of the Symbolic, with humans interpreting, packaging and re-packaging into different forms (see Tran 2013; Yunkaporta and Kirby 2011). This is illustrated by researchers who found teachers can impose very particular views on mathematical constructs such as 'a circle':

In some of the transcripts… it is as if [the teacher] was saying "this is not a circle" - Ceci n'est pas un "circle" - as she pointed to a representation of something seen by her as "circular" but seen by her students as a "circle". But one might ask – what then is a real circle, or even when is a circle, and who decides? What form of authority would one invoke to adjudicate alternative claims? Or rather how might this process of adjudication proceed? And what sorts of things would be offered in evidence? Who would be called as expert defense witnesses? What status would "circle" have at each stage of the proceedings? (Bradford and Brown 2005, p. 5)

We might engage in this analysis as a 'cynic' (or even 'fundamentalist') to argue that this does not apply to the everyday occurrences of classrooms in inner London, Paris, Chicago, or wherever (Žižek 2009, pp. 68–69). But remember Žižek's point that this form of engagement is a source of magical illusion: mathematics education researchers have also acknowledged that the ways of knowing and understanding mathematics have become structured into 'mechanical skills and procedural forms' which can be readily tested in contemporary school settings (Brown and McNamara 2011). Here, "school knowledge derives from administrations trying to administer populations of teachers and children with more or less predictable results against a register of externally defined standards" (Brown and Heywood 2011, p. 365). Specifically:

School mathematics has a tendency to enshrine particular objects (e.g. squares, the first ten integers, the formula for factorising quadratics) or procedures (e.g. the decomposition method of subtraction, iterative processes)… It is often applied mathematics that is shaped around recognizable situations. Particular configurations are repeatedly used resulting in the landscape of mathematics being viewed through perspectives that begin to characterise our engagement with mathematics. Questions are asked in familiar ways. Particular areas of mathematics are favoured, such as the bits that are more easily tested (finding the difference between two integers, finding the area of triangle) rather than exploring a mathematical terrain, say through an investigation. (Brown 2013, p. 6)

So what might it mean to loosen the Symbolic in such mathematics education contexts? Returning to the subject of 'circles', researchers have found more 'exploratory' educative practices which enable learners to experience multiple ways of understanding 'circles':

The mathematical object in question is a circle (or ellipse). Yet the perspectives assumed of this circle obscure its appearance as a clear-cut geometric entity. The task was centred on being able to apprehend an orbit through various projections, such that the students were challenged to situate themselves within and experience mathematically conceived space. The question of moving around this ellipse whilst maintaining the correct orientation further complicates the sharing of perceptions in words… Whatever its correctness, bodily coordination felt like a sound interim step en route to achieving a better understanding… (Walshaw and Brown 2012, p. 194)

Creating a more 'open ended' approach to teaching geometry within a classroom setting, researchers have found that learners can be enabled to make sense of the problem in different but "equally valid" ways including through movement, drawings and equations. Students reported, for example:

...each individual gave very different, but equally valid, explanations. For example, the explanations for seeing a circle in 3D were given as: a penny being spun around at the end of a piece of string; modelling the shape with your hands; imagining being the origin of the circle (therefore being inside the shape) and what it would look like looking in each direction; imagining the shape being built up from the established points which were on the ground. (Brown 2013, p. 10)

But are these experimentations of drawing differently from the Symbolic always limited in how much they can change? Has Žižek not already alerted us to the very limited likelihood that such individual action would actually challenge the wider Symbolic in which we are all engaged in living out on a daily basis? Was this not clear in the examples above: we can change the academic framework within an institution, perhaps altering how we relate to a programme of higher education study, but it does not change the coordinates of how higher education is understood as a bunch of credits in an academic programme (which might be said as the underlying mechanism of how 'halfness' is understood). We can change how we relate to the people within our specific context, such as positioning them as partners rather than clients, but it does not change the wider coordinates of why our job exists in the first place, that is to engage clients on behalf of our employer. And we can change the way we relate to and make sense of even those constructs we believe are fixed, such as a 'circle', but these are unlikely to change wider accepted definitions of 'circle' used by the examiners of the qualification awarding bodies. In other words, it does not change the Symbolic order which keep us securely held and gripped in particular ways of thinking and being.

It might be frustrating for some that Žižek does not give us a definitive guide about what to do to transform education, or more precisely, to tackle the 'troubles in paradise' we are suggesting within the book. Yet, in a dialectical twist, this is also the opportunity for us to apply and assert our own thinking to navigate in different ways and closely examine what we think appears as a result. This is not a 'victory narrative': for Žižek, changing the coordinates of how we understand education takes time, risk, energy, and in ways we may not even be able to articulate right now—and we will certainly and fully tricked en route. We will gaze at the plum to quench our thirst, we will hit the dog with a meat bun to protect ourselves, we will sit on the donkey's back to find it, and we will most certainly cut our noses off to spite our faces.

Perhaps what we can do does return us to the notion of undertaking 'patient ideologico-critical work'. On an individual level, this might mean individuals taking action in their own professional space to reframe and disrupt the way they relate to and experience their professional life—as discussed in the examples above. Here, it is possible through carefully choosing how we draw from the Symbolic, to make different and multiple specific demands over time. Perhaps we could start with playing with two fictions Žižek mentioned earlier: that the constructions generated by the Symbolic and their underlying regulatory power do not exist. How might we act differently if we started playing with alternative notions of education or learning in our specific educational contexts? If mathematics educationalists can experiment with new ways of constructing mathematical knowledge, it seems that it is only our (fictitious) selves that is limiting what we do—recall that wider regulatory influence "exists only insofar as individuals treat it as such, relate to it as such" (Žižek 2006, p. 6). Indeed, Vygotsky referred to the idea of 'serious play' where we take hold of social constructions, an example of what he might call a cultural resource, to work for us, rather than us working 'to the construct' (Vygotsky 1978).

But within the field of practice, it seems that our action is restricted to regaining or reasserting a sense of professional agency within our own context. What this means is that perhaps the broader coordinates of capitalism also needs 'patient ideologico-critical work'. Can the same principle of 'serious play' be applied on a wider scale, where the sector makes specific interventions that have 'ripple effects' challenging commodity relationships and the nostrums generated by them? While necessarily imperfect, perhaps there are already some fertile seeds around us in the form of (genuine) free schools like Summerhill, Montessori schools, or in more 'experimental' Open Educational Resources like MOOCs which do not attempt to fit into a wider system. Also, what about in the arenas for discussion, activist organisations and political groupings that promote these challenging perspectives outside of the formal education system? Perhaps, as a concerted effort, what we need is a more connected attempt to develop and position these approaches as realistic alternatives? But if so, how might we achieve this?

Perhaps alongside changes to individual professional practice, people and organisations can be connected in ways—such as through associations, parties, councils and other bodies—to specifically co-ordinate approaches that challenge the Symbolic coordinates of capitalism?. This is where Žižek himself has playfully argued that a master-signifier and possibly even a 'Master' figure is useful in creating "an authentic division… a division between those who want to drag on within the old parameters and those who are aware of the necessary change" (Žižek 2014a, p. 185). Or in other words, identifying someone—or perhaps something—that can draw differently from the Symbolic realm. That is, divide up the Real in different ways and thereby mobilise new desires and drives in the way described in this book.

Yet as we have already seen, Žižek also reminds us that we are so easily caught in the coordinates of a wider global capitalism, whereby it is not just a community or even a country that lives out particular ideas and beliefs—recall how the Global Learning Qualifications Framework epitomises such a notion (Empire State College 2015). As Žižek says, "one should analyse the capitalist system as a totality of interdependent links" (Žižek 2014b, p. 155), which helps explain why such global forces are able to keep us firmly located within a competition-driven environment that transcends boundaries. Here, for Žižek, the task is to connect common interests across national frontiers to make specific demands towards 'serious play' on a global scale. Here, the "lack of global coordination is acutely felt" (Žižek 2014b, p. 157), and in an especially apposite example of this, Žižek was critical of the vagueness of recent challenges to capitalism such as the Occupy Movement that some have argued otherwise embodied much of this playful, anti-capitalist spirit.

Instead, he has contended that his concept of the 'Master' can play a key role—and in a way which effects how we fundamentally organise society:

A true Master is not an agent of discipline and prohibition. His message is not 'You cannot!', nor 'You have to...!', but a liberating 'You can!'. But 'can' what? Do the impossible, i.e. what appears to be impossible within the coordinates of the existing constellation – and today, this means something very precise: you can think beyond capitalism and liberal democracy as the ultimate framework of our lives. (Žižek 2014b, p. 188)

This goes beyond our own professional practice, it goes beyond education departments and their policies, and it even goes beyond nation states, to encourage intervention in "social and ideological relations which, without necessarily destroying anything or anyone, transforms the entire Symbolic field" (Žižek 2014a, p. 187). And the ever-provocative Žižek has contended this can be facilitated by strong leaders in ways that effectively reconnect his ideas with his Leninist (if not Stalinist) past—at just a period when these ideas had seemed to make way for a more participatory and directly democratic approach from critics of the market economy (Žižek 2013b).

So at this stage of the book, a new set of Žižekian questions for us all might be emerging. Can the 'Master' Žižek speaks of be a master-signifier that transcends notions related to both commodities and even commodified people signified as 'great leaders', and be activated more widely instead? How can this type of concept be used within our professional contexts, which will enable us to challenge practice and mobilise new expectations for the people we engage with? Who might we connect with to bring about these new educational futures? And even more broadly, what global networks might we connect with so as to work with others to inspire a wider, more coherent movement for transformation in society?

As Žižek has conceived and styled the nature of the 'Master', it is easy to see that he may even possibly have himself in mind as a particular academic personification of this very phenomenon: igniting passions and fundamentally dividing people, just like that well-known, intensely salty, yeast extract product. If so, and to return to the joke at the start of this book, where do we now position ourselves in the proverbial lecture theatre? Are we gazing cautiously onto the delights of the performance below, wondering what we are witnessing? Are we gazing cynically on the incompetence and noise of the sights we are seeing? Or have we left the lecture theatre already with a burning desire to answer the emails that demand our attention? These are all understandable responses under contemporary educational circumstances, but they are not acts which can necessarily change educational futures. Alternatively, are we willing to answer Žižek's call to action? And rather than leaving the theatre or checking our emails on our mobile phones—are we stood with the two academics on the lecture theatre stage when the spotlights go out, pulling violently on Žižek's beard?

Only time will tell which of these it is—for while Žižek may have been asking the questions, it is up to us to both provide the answers and act on them.

References

Aitkenhead, D. (2012). *The Guardian - Slavoj Žižek: 'Humanity is OK, but 99 % of people are boring idiots'*. Retrieved March 14, 2015, from http://www.theguardian.com/culture/2012/jun/10/slavoj-zizek-humanity-ok-people-boring.

Barltrop, R. (1975). *The Monument: The story of the Socialist Party of Great Britain*. London: Pluto Press.

Barnett, R. (2000). *Realizing the University in an age of supercomplexity*. Buckingham: Open University/Society for Research into Higher Education.

Barnett, R. (2003). *Beyond all reason: Living with ideology in the University*. London: Society for Research into Higher Education.

Barnett, R. (2011). The coming of the ecological University. *Oxford Review of Education, 37*(4), 439–455.

Bolden, R., Connor, H., Duquemin, A., Hirsh, W., & Petrov, G. (2009). *Employer engagement with higher education: Defining, sustaining, and supporting higher skills provision*. London: Department for Innovation, Universities and Skills.

Bourdieu, P. (1988). *Homo academicus*. Cambridge: Polity Press.

Bradford, K., & Brown, T. (2005). C'est n'est pas un circle. *For the Learning of Mathematics, 25*(1), 16–19.

Brown, T. (2008). Desire and drive in researcher subjectivity: The broken mirror of Lacan. *Qualitative Inquiry, 14*(2), 402–423.

Brown, T. (2013). *The sublime objects of mathematics in schools*. Paper presented at the mathematics education and contemporary theory conference, 21st–24th June.

Brown, T., Atkinson, D., & England, J. (2006). *Regulative discourses in education: A Lacanian perspective*. London: Peter Lang Publishers.

Brown, T., & England, J. (2005). Identity, narrative and practitioner research: A Lacanian perspective. *Discourse: Studies in the Cultural Politics of Education, 26*(4), 443–458.

Brown, T., & Heywood, D. (2011). Geometry, subjectivity and the seduction of language: The regulation of spatial perception. *Educational Studies in Mathematics, 7*, 351–367.

Brown, T., & Jones, L. (2001). *Action research and postmodernism: Congruence and critique*. Milton Keynes: Open University Press.

Brown, T., & McNamara, O. (2011). *Becoming a mathematics teacher: Identity and identifications*. Dordrecht: Springer.

Brown, T., & Walshaw, M. (2012). Mathematics education and contemporary theory. *Educational Studies in Mathematics, 80*(1–2), 1–8.

Butler, R. (2005). *Slavoj Žižek: Live Theory*. London: Continuum.

Chahine, I., & Kinuthia, W. (2013). Juxtaposing form function, and social symbolism: An ethnomathematical analysis of Indigenous technologies in the Zulu culture. *Journal of Mathematics & Culture, 7*(1), 1–30.

Cooley, A. (2009). Is education a lost cause? Žižek, schooling, and universal emancipation. *Discourse: Studies in the Cultural Politics of Education, 30*(4), 381–395.

Empire State College. (2015). *The global learning qualifications framework*. Retrieved March 15, 2015, from http://www.esc.edu/suny-real/global-learning-qualifications-framework/.

England, J. (2003). Researching race in school: A psychoanalytical perspective. Manchester Metropolitan University.

For Dummies. (2015). *For dummies [Homepage]*. Retrieved March 14, 2015, from http://www.dummies.com/.

Foucault, M. (1980). Power/Knowledge. In C. Gordon (Ed.), *Selected interviews and other writings 1972-77* (pp. 170–194). Brighton: Harvester.

Furedi, F. (2006). *Where have all the intellectuals gone? Confronting 21st Century Philistinism* (2nd ed.). London: Continuum.

Furedi, F. (2010). *Wasted: Why education isn't educating*. London: Continuum.

Greenstreet, R. (2008). *The Guardian Q&A: Slavoj Žižek, professor and writer*. Retrieved March 14, 2015, from http://www.theguardian.com/lifeandstyle/2008/aug/09/slavoj.zizek.

Habermas, J. (1976). Systematically distorted communication. In P. Connerton (Ed.), *Critical Sociology*. Harmondsworth: Penguin.

Kaino, L. M. (2013). Traditional knowledge in curricula designs: Embracing indigenous mathematics in classroom instruction. *Studies of Tribes and Tribals, 11*(1), 83–88.

Mariborchan.si. (2014). *Slavoj Zizek - Education, Tutors, Universities, Students*. Retrieved October10, 2014, from http://mariborchan.si/video/recordings/slavoj-zizek/slavoj-zizek-education-tutors-universities-students/.

Meakin, D., & Wall, T. (2013). Co-delivered work based learning: Contested ownership and responsibility. *Higher Education, Skills & Work Based Learning, 3*(1), 73–81.

Pais, A. (2011). *Mathematics education and the political: An ideology critique of an educational research field*. Unpublished Doctoral Thesis, Aalborg Universitet, Aalborg.

Perrin, D. (2000). *The Socialist Party of Great Britain: Politics, economics and Britain's oldest socialist party*. Wrexham: Bridge Books.

Ricoeur, P. (1984). *Time and narrative* (Vol. 1). Chicago: Chicago University Press.

Rose, J. (2002). *The intellectual life of the British working classes*. New Haven, CT: Yale University Press.

Schuman, R. (2014). *Slate—Please stop worshipping the Superstar Professor who calls students "Boring Idiots"*. Retrieved March 14, 2015, from http://www.slate.com/blogs/browbeat/2014/06/02/slavoj_zizek_calls_students_stupid_and_boring_stop_worshiping_this_man_video.html.

Smith, K., Hodson, E., & Brown, T. (2013). Teacher educator changing perceptions of theory. *Educational Action Research, 21*(2), 237–252.

Steele, T. (2015). Enlightened publics: Popular education movements in Europe, their legacy and promise. *Studies in the Education of Adults, 42*(2), 107–123.

Taylor, P. (2010). *Žižek and the Media*. Cambridge: Polity Press.

Tran, L. T. (2013). *Teaching international students in vocational education: New pedagogical approaches*. Camberwell: Australian Council for Educational Research.

Vasagar, J., & Smithers, R. (2003). *The Guardian—Will Charles Clarke have his place in history?* Retrieved March 14, 2015, from http://www.theguardian.com/uk/2003/may/10/highereducation.politics.

Vygotsky, L. S. (1978). *Mind in society: The Development of higher psychological processes*. Cambridge, MA: Harvard University Press.

Wall, T. (2013). *Professional identities and commodification in higher education*. Unpublished Doctoral Thesis, Manchester Metropolitan University, Manchester.

Walshaw, M., & Brown, T. (2012). Affective productions of mathematical experience. *Educational Studies in Mathematics, 80*(1–2), 185–199. doi:10.1007/s10649-011-9370-x.

Wedgewood, M. (2008). *Higher education for the workforce—Barriers and facilitators to employer engagement*. London: Department for Innovation, Universities and Skills.

Wolters, E. (2014). *Critical Theory - Professor of the year, "if you don't give me any of your shitty papers you get an A"*. Retrieved March 14, 2015, from http://www.critical-theory.com/professor-of-the-year-if-you-dont-give-me-any-of-your-shitty-papers-you-get-an-a/.

Yunkaporta, T., & Kirby, M. (2011). Yarning up indigenous pedagogies: A dialogue about eight aboriginal ways of learning. In N. Purdie, G. Milgate, & H. R. Bell (Eds.), *Two way teaching and learning: Toward culturally reflective and relevant education*. Camberwell: Australian Council for Educational Research.

Žižek, S. (1989). *The sublime object of ideology*. London: Verso.

Žižek, S. (1994). The spectre of ideology. In S. Žižek (Ed.), *Mapping ideology* (pp. 1–33). London: Verso.

Žižek, S. (1999). *The ticklist subject: The absent centre of political ontology* (2008 Verso ed.). London: Verso.

Žižek, S. (2002). *Enjoy your symptom! Jacques Lacan in Hollywood and out* (2nd ed.). London: Routledge.

Žižek, S. (2006). *The parallax view*. Cambridge, MA: MIT Press.

Žižek, S. (2009). *First as tragedy, then as farce*. London: Verso.

Žižek, S. (2010). A permanent economic emergency. *New Left Review, 64,* 85–95.

Žižek, S. (2013a). *Denial: The Liberal Utopia*. Retrieved January 17, from, http://www.lacan.com/essays/?page_id=397.

Žižek, S. (2013b). *The New Statesman—The simple courage of decision: A leftist tribute to Thatcher*.   http://www.newstatesman.com/politics/politics/2013/04/simple-courage-decision-leftist-tribute-thatcher.

Žižek, S. (2014a). *Event*. London: Penguin.

Žižek, S. (2014b). *Trouble in paradise: from the end of history to the end of capitalism*. London: Allen Lane.

Chapter 7
Springboard Resources

Abstract Žižek's words, and others' words about him and his work, are readily available in many forms, from short, online video clips to extensive theoretical works. The resources listed in this chapter are some springboards to learning more about the man and his work.

Starting with Žižek: Žižek's book *Event: Philosophy in Transit* (published by Penguin in 2014) offers one of the easier reads, but it does not explicitly detail the underpinning theory. For this, it might be useful to revisit the classic *The Sublime Object of Ideology* (published by Verso in 1989, with a new edition appearing in 2009), or *The Parallax View* (published by MIT Press in 2006). Žižek's *Trouble in Paradise: From the End of History to the End of Capitalism* (also published by Penguin in 2014) provides applications of his thinking to more recent events, with occasional but cursory mention of students and education.

Keeping informed with Žižek: The Guardian newspaper's profile of Žižek provides an evolving commentary of social affairs (http://www.theguardian.com/profile/slavojzizek). A posting directly relevant to education may appear here soon! In addition, the European Graduate School's profile of Žižek also provides a useful overview of Žižek's history and publications (http://www.egs.edu/faculty/slavoj-zizek/biography/).

'How to read' kind of books related to Žižek: There are many of these books to flick through, each providing a slightly different angle of the man and his work. Examples include: *Žižek: A Guide for the Perplexed*, by Sean Sheehan, published by Continuum in 2012; *Slavoj Žižek: A Critical Introduction*, by Ian Parker, published by Pluto Press in 2004. One of the most engaging is *Žižek's Jokes: Did you hear the one about Hegel and negation?*, written by Žižek but compiled and edited by Audun Mortensen, published by MIT Press in 2014.

Applications of Žižek: The International Journal of Žižek Studies, also called IJŽS, is a peer-reviewed, open access academic journal with over 14,000 subscribers. See http://www.zizekstudies.org/, but it is also available through Facebook https://www.facebook.com/groups/Zizekstudies/. Articles with a Žižekian flavour also appear in the *Journal of Unschooling and Alternative Learning* (http://jual.nipissingu.ca/) also called JUAL. And finally, the Ke$ha and Žižek Tumblr page

© The Author(s) 2015

T. Wall and D. Perrin, *Slavoj Žižek*,

SpringerBriefs on Key Thinkers in Education,

DOI 10.1007/978-3-319-21242-5_7

(http://keshek.tumblr.com/) provides a juxtaposition of contemporary pop singer and quotes from Žižek, through the medium of 'animated gifs' (which are animations lasting a few seconds). Strange, but provides illustrative of how his quotes or ideas might be applied to unexpected situations.

Printed by Printforce, the Netherlands